Effective Vocabulary

D. J. Henry
Daytona Beach Community College

Susan Pongratz
Thomas Nelson Community College

New York   Boston   San Francisco
London Toronto Sydney Tokyo Singapore Madrid
Mexico City Munich Paris Cape Town Hong Kong Montreal

Senior Acquisitions Editor: Melanie Craig
Development Editor: Susan Gouijnstook
Marketing Manager: Thomas DeMarco
Senior Supplements Editor: Donna Campion
Media Supplements Editor: Jenna Egan
Production Manager: Ellen MacElree
Project Coordination, Text Design, and Electronic Page Makeup: Nesbitt Graphics, Inc.
Cover Design Manager: Wendy Ann Fredericks
Cover Designer: Joe DePinho
Photo Researcher: Rona Tuccillo
Senior Manufacturing Buyer: Dennis J. Para
Printer and Binder: Worldcolor–Taunton
Cover Printer: Phoenix Color Corps

Library of Congress Cataloging-in-Publication Data on file with the Library of Congress

Please visit us at http://www.ablongman.com/vocabulary

ISBN 0-321-41071-8 (Student Edition)

ISBN 0-321-43448-X (Instructor's Edition)

5 6 7 8 9 10—WCT—09

Contents

UNIT 5
Vocabulary in Communications and Humanities   190

APPENDIXES

Preface

Learning new vocabulary requires preparation and practice. Most students add 2,000 to 3,000 words each year to their reading vocabularies. A knowledge of vocabulary is closely tied to a student's reading comprehension, and college textbooks contain a great deal of specialized vocabulary; therefore, increasing your vocabulary through the study of context clues, word analysis, and dictionary practice will improve your ability to comprehend and communicate.

The chapters in this textbook contain features to provide several encounters with each new word to promote in-depth learning.

Get Ready to Read About

Each chapter begins with an introduction that includes information about a college course and the word parts to help you understand the vocabulary of that subject area.

Vocabulary in Context

We learn most of our vocabulary by watching, listening, and reading, and you will discover in Chapter 1 that recognizing context clues will facilitate your learning. Therefore, unless you are directed to do so, please avoid using a dictionary. However, after you have completed the first exercise, turn to the partial answer key to check your answers.

Synonyms and Antonyms

Each chapter includes an exercise on synonyms and antonyms. Learning a one-word definition (synonym) and learning the opposite meaning (antonym) will provide practice with what the word is and what it is not.

Stop and Think

At the end of each chapter, you will find two exercises to help you learn the new words. Whether you are asked to use the words to write a summary or search online for additional information about the word, each activity is designed so that you can work alone or in a study group. Remember, if you encounter the word seven or eight times, you are more likely to remember its definition and the correct way to use it.

The Teaching and Learning Package

Longman is pleased to offer a variety of support materials to help make teaching vocabulary easier on teachers and to help students excel in their coursework. Contact your local Longman sales representative for more information on pricing and how to create a package.

An **Annotated Instructor's Edition (0-321-43448-X)** is available to Instructors. The Annotated Instructor's Edition is an exact replica of the student edition with the answers included.

Vocabulary Skills Study Card (Student/ 0-321-31802-1)
Colorful, affordable, and packed with useful information, Longman's Vocabulary Study Card is a concise, 8-page reference guide to developing key vocabulary skills, such as learning to recognize context clues, reading a dictionary entry, and recognizing key root words, suffixes, and prefixes. Laminated for durability, students can keep this Study Card for years to come and pull it out whenever they need a quick review.

Oxford American College Dictionary (Student / 0-399-14415-3)
A hard cover reference with more than 175,000.

The New American Webster Handy College Dictionary
(Student / 0-451-18166-2)
A paperback reference text with more than 100,000 entries.

Multimedia Offerings

Interested in incorporating online materials into your course? Longman is happy to help. Our regional technology specialists provide training on all of our multimedia offerings.

MyReadingLab (www.myreadinglab.com)
This exciting new website houses all the media tools any developmental English student will need to improve their reading and study skills, and all in one easy to use place.

Other Books in This Series

Book 1: Developing Vocabulary (0-321-41070-X)
Book 3: Mastering Vocabulary (0-321-41072-6)

Acknowledgments

We are indebted to the many reviewers for their invaluable contributions. We would especially like to thank the following reviewers for their suggestions and guidance: Bonnie Bailey, Arapahoe Community College; Jennifer Britton, Valencia Community College West; Flo J. Hill, Albany State University; Jocelyn Jacobs, Lee College; Evelyn Koperwas, Broward Community College; Carrie Phyrr, Austin Community College; Sharette Simpkins, Florida Community College at Jacksonville; Wendy Wish, Valencia Community College; and Lynda Wolverton, Polk Community College.

Many people have helped make this project a gratifying journey. My campus colleague and good friend Mary Dubbé emboldened me to persevere. I thank her for balance, direction, and encouragement. My best virtual friend Janet Elder provided inspiration and levity in some of the most uncanny and well-timed communications. The connection is inexplicably delightful. For the artwork and photographs, I thank Molly Gamble-Walker, Gabrielle Fletcher, Charles Correll, Susan Gouijnstook, George Pongratz, and Elizabeth Pongratz. May their muses continue to provide. I am grateful for the patience, suggestions, and gracious attention from my editor Susan Gouijnstook, who continues to give me courage in the quietest of ways. Thanks also to Melanie Craig, acquisitions editor, Ellen MacElree, senior production editor, and Rona Tucillo, visual research manager. Finally, I gratefully acknowledge the talented and incomparable Kathy Smith for scrutinizing, sifting, raking, editing, proofing, fixing, polishing, and encouraging me during the writing of this book.

—Susan Pongratz

It is such a thrill to partner with Susan Pongratz, a gifted teacher and writer, to provide this comprehensive vocabulary program. It is so gratifying to work with a kindred spirit who shares a deep devotion to students and clear vision for their academic success. In talent, creativity, and dedication, none can compare to Susan Pongratz, and I thank her for giving so much of herself. I would also like to thank Susan Gouijnstook, Developmental Editor, and Melanie Craig, Acquisition Editor, for their faith in our work. Finally, I would like to thank all of you who allow us to partner with you in your classroom instruction. It is an honor to be a part of your life's work!

—D. J. Henry

STUDY Tips

Throughout this book, you will be asked to practice using and working with new words. By creating study cards, you will enhance your in-depth knowledge of the words. Study the models to determine new ways of learning vocabulary.

Frayer Model

To complete a modified Frayer Model, follow these steps.
Write the word in the center of the card.

1. Definition/synonyms (one-word definitions) of the word.
2. Write characteristics or other forms of the word.
3. Write the antonyms.
4. Write a non-example (people, things, descriptions of what the word is not).

Definition/Synonyms	Characteristics
Vocabulary Word	
Antonyms	Non-examples

Example 1

Synonyms friendly, genial, cordial, hospitable	**Characteristics** fun-loving, laughter, smiles
	convivial	
Antonyms unfriendly, dull, grim, antisocial	**Non-examples** Grim Reaper, Hannibal Lecter, Wicked Witch of the West

Example 2

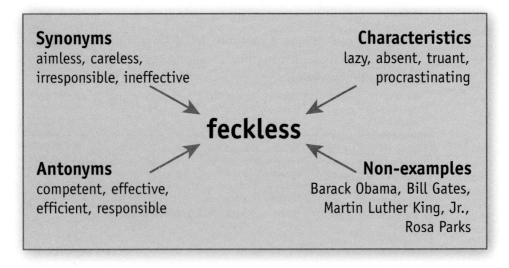

Synonyms
aimless, careless,
irresponsible, ineffective

Characteristics
lazy, absent, truant,
procrastinating

feckless

Antonyms
competent, effective,
efficient, responsible

Non-examples
Barack Obama, Bill Gates,
Martin Luther King, Jr.,
Rosa Parks

Visual Vocabulary Cards

Another way to learn new vocabulary words is to create cards with sketches or pictures to help you visualize the word and the definition. For example, to learn the word *incongruous,* which means *out of place* or *inconsistent,* imagine a little dog with a name and accessories that are not consistent or expected with his size. Therefore, you could connect the word and the image.

Example

Incongruous (ĭn-kŏng′grōō-əs) adj.

Out of place; inconsistent

The oversized bone and house are as **incongruous** as the little dog's name, Big Boy.

Molly Gamble-Walker

Pyramid Summary

1. Write the vocabulary word.
2. List three synonyms (one-word definitions).
3. List the word parts and definitions (if available).
4. List antonyms (opposites) of the word.
5. Write a sentence using the word.

Paradox
contradiction, catch-22, enigma
para = contradictory, dox = opinion
Antonyms: legality, edict, equation, verdict, judgment, decision
A paradox of life is that you have to have money to make money.

KIM

Divide the index card into three columns.

1. Write the vocabulary word in column 1.
2. Write any information you have about the word, such as the definition, synonyms, antonyms, and a sentence in column 2.
3. Create a drawing that represents the word in column 3.

Key Word	Information	Mental Image
Write the vocabulary word.	Write the definition, synonym, antonym, sentence.	Draw a picture.

Example

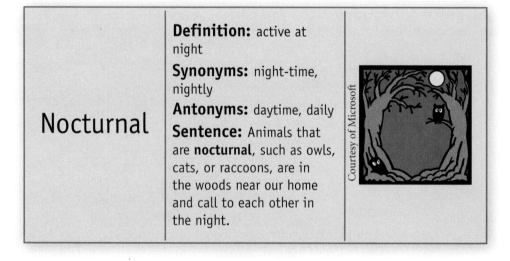

Nocturnal

Definition: active at night

Synonyms: night-time, nightly

Antonyms: daytime, daily

Sentence: Animals that are **nocturnal**, such as owls, cats, or raccoons, are in the woods near our home and call to each other in the night.

Courtesy of Microsoft

1

Using Context Clues and Word Analysis

Get Ready to Read About Context Clues and Word Analysis

A good vocabulary is one of the elements of academic success. Adding to your personal inventory of words is an ongoing process that requires knowledge of context clues and word parts. As you read through this chapter, consider your prior knowledge about the following words:

Vocabulary—the words used or understood by a person

Context clue—information that surrounds a new word and is used to understand its meaning

Synonym—a word that has the same or nearly the same meaning as another word

Antonym—a word that has the opposite meaning of another word

Prefix—a group of letters with a specific meaning that is added to the beginning of a word to form a new word

Root—the foundation of a word

Suffix—a group of letters with a specific meaning that is added to the end of a word to form a new meaning (Suffixes may also change the part of speech of a word.)

"Lorsque j'avais six ans j'ai vu, une fois, une magnifique image, dans un livre sur la forêt vierge qui s'appelait *Histoires vécues*. Ca représentait un serpent boa qui avalait un fauve. Voilà la copie du dessin."

—Excerpt and illustration from *Le Petit Prince* by Antoine de Saint-Exupéry, copyright 1943 by Harcourt, Inc. and renewed 1971 by Consuelo de Saint-Exupéry, reprinted by permission of the publisher.

When Elizabeth tried to translate this paragraph from *Le Petit Prince* by Antoine de Saint-Exupéry, without the necessary background knowledge in French, she remarked, "I could do a whole lot better if I knew the vocabulary. It's so critical to understanding everything!"

Here is the translation:

"Once when I was six I saw a magnificent picture in a book about the jungle, called *True Stories*. It showed a boa constrictor swallowing a wild beast. Here is a copy of the picture."

—Excerpt from *The Little Prince* by Antoine de Saint-Exupéry, copyright 1943 by Harcourt, Inc. and renewed 1971 by Consuelo de Saint-Exupéry, English translation copyright © 2000 by Richard Howard, reprinted by permission of Harcourt, Inc.

Words Are Building Blocks

Looking at the anecdote about Elizabeth reading her French homework, you can see that learning vocabulary is critical to understanding. Many college courses use specialized vocabulary, and sometimes it seems as if these words are in a foreign language. Increasing your personal vocabulary also requires that you begin with a foundation. Think of each word as a building block of meaning. Developing an understanding of simple words enables you to comprehend other more complex words. Building a large inventory of vocabulary words enhances your communication skills, which leads to academic success.

Vocabulary is all the words used or understood by a person.

How many words do you have in your vocabulary? At the age of 4, you only knew about 5,600 words. By the age of 10, you had increased that number to about 34,000 words. If you are like most people, by the time you are 18 years old, you know about 60,000 words. In one college year, however, you will double that to 120,000 words. During your entire college studies, you will most likely learn an additional 20,000 words. Each subject you study will have its own set of words.*

There are several ways to study vocabulary, and we will examine them in the following sections.

Vocabulary in Context

Effective college students interact with new words in a number of ways. One way is to use context clues. The meaning of a word is shaped by its context. The word *context* means "surroundings." Effective readers use context clues to learn new words.

> A **context clue** is the information that surrounds a new word and is used to understand its meaning.

The four most common types of context clues are:

- Synonyms
- Antonyms
- General context
- Examples

Notice that, put together, the first letter of each context clue spells the word **SAGE.** The word *sage* means "wise." Using context clues is a wise—or **SAGE**—reading strategy, and this mnemonic device, or memory trick, will help you recall the kinds of context clues writers use.

Synonyms

A **synonym** is a word that has the same or nearly the same meaning as another word. You can remember this because the prefix *syn-* means *same* and the root *nym* means *name*. For example, the words *erudite* and *scholarly* are synonyms because they both have similar meanings. Many times, an author will place a synonym near a new or difficult word to provide a context clue to the word's meaning. Usually, a synonym is set off with a pair of commas, dashes, or parentheses before and after it, or it is introduced by a signal word.

Synonym Signal Words
or   that is

---

*http://www.ucc.vt.edu/stdysk/vocabula.html retrieved 11/01/2005 and Henry, D.J., *The Effective Reader*.

Gas prices have become **exorbitant**; that is, they are excessively high.

Exorbitant means _____

   a. affordable.
   b. expensive.
   c. tall.
   d. cruel.

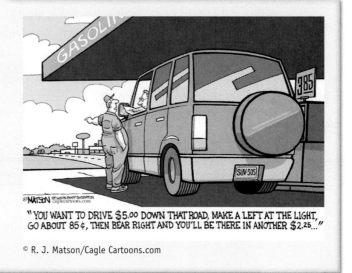

" YOU WANT TO DRIVE $5.⁰⁰ DOWN THAT ROAD, MAKE A LEFT AT THE LIGHT, GO ABOUT 85¢, THEN BEAR RIGHT AND YOU'LL BE THERE IN ANOTHER $2.25..."

© R. J. Matson/Cagle Cartoons.com

Antonyms

An **antonym** is a word that has the opposite meaning of another word. For example, *initiate* (to begin) and *terminate* (to end) are antonyms. Antonyms help you see the shade of a word's meaning by showing you what the original word is *not.* The following contrast words often act as signals that an antonym is being used.

Antonym Signal Words		
although	but	conversely
despite	however	in contrast
instead	nevertheless	not
on the other hand	whereas	yet

Sometimes antonyms can be found next to the new word. In those cases, commas, dashes, or parentheses set them off. At other times, antonyms are placed in other parts of the sentence to emphasize the contrast between the ideas.

General Context

Often you will find that the author has not provided either a synonym or an antonym clue. In that case, you will have to rely on the general context of the passage to figure out the meaning of the unfamiliar word. This requires you to read the entire sentence, or to read ahead for the next few sentences, for information that will help you understand the new word.

Information about the word can be included in the passage in several ways. In many cases, a definition of the word is presented. Vivid word pictures or descriptions of a situation can provide a sense of the word's meaning. Sometimes you may need to figure out the meaning of an unknown word by using logic and reasoning skills based on your personal experience and background knowledge.

Examples

Many times an author will show the meaning of a new or difficult word by providing an example. Signal words indicate that an example is coming.

Example Signal Words				
for instance	*for example*	*such as*	*including*	*consists of*

Colons and dashes can also indicate examples.

In addition to using context clues for vocabulary improvement, an effective reader will study visual images and captions provided in textbooks. Likewise, a good reader will study graphs, charts, photographs, and cartoons.*

VISUAL VOCABULARY

At the conclusion of their college experience, new graduates have great **aspirations,** such as landing exciting jobs, traveling to interesting places, and enjoying new adventures.

Aspiration means _____

  a. height.   c. difficulty.
  b. dream.   d. dissatisfaction.

Jeff Koterba, Omaha World Herald, NE
Reprinted with permission: North America Syndicate.

*"Clues," by D.J. Henry from *The Skilled Reader*, pp. 45–57.

SAGE

Context Clue	Example	Definition
Synonym	Oregon is **adjacent,** or next to, California and Washington.	near; next to; bordering
Antonym	Grandma was becoming **senile**, but Grandpa was still mentally alert and sharp.	forgetful as a result of age
General Context	Our 90-year-old Uncle John is a **venerable** relative, but his selfish twin brother Victor is only worthy of our disrespect.	worthy of respect because of being older
Example	Donna's **genial** brother tells jokes, coaches his children's sports teams, and always makes people feel welcome.	friendly

EXERCISE 1 Synonym Clues

A. Select the letter of the best definition for the word in **bold** print.

1. My cousin is **eccentric**, but the odd things he does seem charming to most people.

_____ **Eccentric** means
a. shy.
b. unusual.
c. lost.
d. simple

2. Ben was **cognizant** that his girlfriend was a well-known flirt, but he was also aware that she was always faithful to him.

_____ **Cognizant** means
a. famous.
b. quiet.
c. aware.
d. forceful.

3. Andrew is on a **quest,** or search, for a simple, uncomplicated life in the mountains.

   _____ **Quest** means

       a. exhaustion.   c. plan.

       b. message.   d. hunt.

4. The new gymnasium is so small that the bleachers closely **abut** (border) the basketball court.

   _____ **Abut** means

       a. be next to.   c. put off.

       b. lie above.   d. receive.

5. Because Molly is a vegan, she **abstains** (that is, voluntarily does without) any meat or animal products such as milk, eggs, or cheese.

   _____ **Abstain** means

       a. do without voluntarily.   c. promise.

       b. touch.   d. enjoy.

B. Fill in the blank with the meaning of the word in **bold** print.

6. Alana is so **mercenary** and greedy that she only chooses to be friends with people who have money.

   Mercenary means _____.

7. The public relations firm studied ways to **disseminate**—that is, send—information about the new company to leaders of the community.

   Disseminate means _____.

8. The new puppy was lively but **docile**, or easy to manage, and the children bonded with it immediately.

   Docile means _____.

9. Alexis was the Alpha female in her group, and she enjoyed the attention of her **minions**—those friends who chose to be her servants just to be a member of the "right" crowd.

   Minion means _____.

10. Kim was always **compliant** and agreeable, never losing her temper and always willing to get along with others.

    Compliant means _____.

EXERCISE **2** Antonym Clues

A. Select the letter of the best definition for the word in **bold** print.

1. Jimmy approaches each morning with **alacrity;** however, his roommate Zach is gloomy and without cheer until after lunch.

_____ **Alacrity** means
a. dull anger.
b. gloomy silence.
c. cheerful enthusiasm.
d. hopeless disappointment.

2. The **prelude** of the play was boring, but the audience was spellbound by the end.

_____ **Prelude** means
a. intermission.
b. introduction.
c. ending.
d. commercial.

3. Ella's car, though an old model, is always **immaculate**; on the other hand, her brother Abram's truck is filthy and always in need of a good vacuuming.

_____ **Immaculate** means
a. clean.
b. dirty.
c. rusty.
d. quiet.

4. After six weeks of exercising, Gina looked **salubrious**; however, her husband, who had not been working out with her, still looked as unhealthy as ever.

_____ **Salubrious** means
a. lonely.
b. sad.
c. tired.
d. healthy.

5. Anthony steadily **tapered** his training schedule as the swim meet approached, but his teammates drastically slowed down their practice sessions.

_____ **Taper** means
a. gradually decrease.
b. quickly increase.
c. drop suddenly.
d. increase suddenly.

B. Fill in the blank with the meaning of the word in **bold** print.

6. After the divorce, Charlie had no **animosity** toward his ex-wife; instead, he felt only good will.

Animosity means _____.

EXERCISE ◢ Example Clues

A. Select the letter of the best definition for the word in **bold** print.

1. Acts of **altruism**—volunteering, collecting donations, supporting charities—remind us of the goodness in humanity.

_____ **Altruism** means

    a. selfishness.   c. criticism.

    b. cruelty.   d. unselfishness.

2. Roger was **intent** on finishing his painting project before the weekend ended, so he worked through the night without taking out time to sleep or eat.

_____ **Intent** means

    a. adventurous.   c. determined.

    b. shy.   d. angry.

3. Whereas Sam preferred studying Renaissance artists, Naomi was a modernist who was interested in **contemporary** American artists such as Jackson Pollock and Edward Hopper.

_____ **Contemporary** means

    a. modern.   c. old-fashioned.

    b. satisfied.   d. patient.

4. Some **lucrative** career fields for recent college graduates include business and engineering, with a starting accountant's salary averaging about $46,000 a year.

_____ **Lucrative** means

    a. easy.   c. determined.

    b. profitable.   d. awkward.

5. "**Poignant** movies that consist of romantic tension between star-crossed lovers always make me sad," moaned Lisa, as she reached for the box of tissues.

_____ **Poignant** means

    a. dangerous.   c. tender; emotional.

    b. boring.   d. expensive.

B. Fill in the blank with the meaning of the word in **bold** print.

6. The sudden increase in home prices was as **incomprehensible** to Ethan as the calculus and quantum mechanics he was struggling with in his classes.

Incomprehensible means ——————————————.

7. The **contour** of the millionaire's home matched the outline of the Pacific coastline.

Contour means ——————————————.

8. Big Foot and the Loch Ness Monster may be **aberrations** of nature, examples of active imaginations, or very clever marketing tricks.

Aberration means ——————————————.

9. Because of technological advances and new imaging techniques, we now know that the brain is **malleable,** much like plastic or clay—something that can be shaped and improved with active stimulation.

Malleable means ——————————————.

10. College athletics is becoming more **sordid** as we hear about athletes who are given special treatment or valuable gifts and who also are able to avoid conviction for unlawful acts.

Sordid means ——————————————.

EXERCISE 5 Vocabulary in Context

A. Select the letter of the best definition for the word in **bold** print.

1. Because of the **complexity** of the Sudoku games in the new book, Ashley was unable to complete the puzzles as quickly as she had in the book with simpler puzzles.

——— **Complexity** means
   a. ease.
   b. difficulty
   c. moderation.
   d. eagerness.

2. When Simon received an extension on his project, he wrote to thank his professor for his patience by saying, "You have been most gracious, and I appreciate your **forbearance.**"

——— **Forbearance** means
   a. disinterest.
   b. impatience.
   c. patience.
   d. discipline.

3. It is always wise to **scrutinize** the fine print in a car warranty, service contract, or insurance policy.

   _____ **Scrutinize** means
   - a. examine.
   - b. write.
   - c. arrange.
   - d. ignore.

4. After cutting down the maple tree, Mitch had to saw the **unwieldy** branches so that they were manageable enough for him to move to the street.

   _____ **Unwieldy** means
   - a. unhealthy.
   - b. easy.
   - c. unmanageable.
   - d. graceful.

5. As a freshman, Jeff was a **zany** cast member—always making silly comments and performing wacky practical jokes; however, by the time he was a senior, he had become a serious and focused actor.

   _____ **Zany** means
   - a. serious.
   - b. unkind.
   - c. calm.
   - d. crazy.

B. Fill in the blank with the meaning of the word in **bold** print.

6. The local fire department recently experienced **unethical** treatment when the city council changed its mind and refused to give the fire fighters the raise they had been promised.

   Unethical means _____.

7. The entertainment for the evening was provided by a talented **a cappella** group of male vocalists, whose singing sound effects proved that musical instruments are not always a required accompaniment.

   A capella means _____.

8. Smokers do not realize how unpleasant the **acrid**—that is, bitter—smell of stale cigarettes is to a nonsmoker.

   Acrid means _____.

9. No matter how much he disagreed with someone, my grandfather would never **slander** or gossip about his neighbors or colleagues.

   Slander means _____.

10. Before the holiday weekend, the local police announced that they set up several check points to encourage **sobriety,** persuading motorists to avoid drinking and driving.

Sobriety means _____.

Word Analysis

Just as ideas are made up of words, words are also made up of smaller parts. Studying word parts can help you learn vocabulary more easily and quickly. In addition, knowing the meaning of the parts of words helps you figure out the meaning of a new word when you first encounter it. It can also help you memorize the definition. Finally, learning word parts can help you improve your spelling ability when you are writing. In fact, the word *misspell* is a combination of the prefix *mis-*, which means *wrong*, and the root *spell*. Many words are divided into the following three parts: roots, prefixes, and suffixes.

Study the chart below to see the role word parts play in vocabulary development by considering the parts of the word *telepathic*, which means *characteristic of communicating feelings from far away*.

Root	Foundation of the word	*path*	feeling
Prefix	Found at the beginning of a word	*tele-*	far
Suffix	Found at the end of a word	*-ic*	characteristic of, like

Root Words

The roots of words form the foundation. Many of our root words come from Latin and Greek words. Learning to recognize the roots of words will help you understand the meanings of many new words.

EXAMPLE   Write the root and meanings of the following words:

deflect, flex, flexible, flexor, genuflect, inflection, inflexibility, reflect, reflex

_____

_____

_____

EXPLANATION   Each of the words has the root *flex*, which comes from the Latin word that means *bend*. By adding a prefix, another root, or a suffix to that foundation, new words are formed.

VISUAL VOCABULARY

Study the cartoon below and then answer the question that follows it.

©Brian Basset. Distributed by The Washington Post Writers Group.

_____ *Telepathically* means

a. communicate slowly.
b. communicate unclearly.

c. communicate from a distance.
d. communicate only with animals.

EXERCISE 1 Root Words

Study the following words and their definitions to determine the meaning of each root:

1. acrophobia: fear of heights
    agoraphobia: fear of open spaces
    monophobia: fear of being alone

    _____ *Phobia* means
    a. life.
    b. fear.

    c. level.
    d. single.

2. biography: story of a person's life
    biology: study of life
    biodegradable: able to be decomposed by small living organisms

    _____ *Bio* means
    a. fear.
    b. small things.

    c. life.
    d. story.

3. generate: cause to come into existence
genealogy: study of a family line
genocide: deliberate killing of a race or culture

_____ *Gen* means

   a. study.

   b. race; kind.

   c. sister or brother.

   d. difference.

4. anarchy: absence or rule or order
hierarchy: body of ranked rulers
archaeology: study of ancient people

_____ *Arch* means

   a. artist, writer.

   b. design.

   c. ruler; first.

   d. elder; servant.

5. affidavit: sworn statement to be trusted
confident: having faith in oneself
perfidy: a violation of faith or trust

_____ *Fid* means

   a. statement.

   b. law.

   c. faith.

   d. violation.

6. fluctuate: to move up and down
reflux: flow backward
flux: continuous flow; flood

_____ *Fluct, flux* mean

   a. flow.

   b. water.

   c. liquid.

   d. travel.

7. finale: ending
finite: that which has an end
finish: to end

_____ *Fin* means

   a. beginning.

   b. end.

   c. first.

   d. separate.

8. gratitude: thankfulness
gratify: to make thankful
ingratiate: to gain favor

_____ *Grat* means

   a. thankful; pleasing.

   b. selfish.

   c. crowded.

   d. alone.

9. convene: to assemble
intervene: to get involved
ventilate: circulate air

_____ *Ven* means
   a. leave.   c. depart.
   b. come.   d. ignore.

10. bellicose: inclined to start quarrels or wars
belligerent: argumentative
antebellum: before the Civil War

_____ *Belli-* means
   a. beauty.   c. peace.
   b. history.   d. war.

EXERCISE 2 Root Words

Study the chart below and insert a second example of a word that contains each root.

Root Words Guide

Root	Definition	Example	Example
aster	star	disaster	_____
bio	life	biology	_____
crypt	hidden	cryptologist	_____
demos	people	democracy	_____
derm	skin	dermatology	_____
fact	make, do	manufacture	_____
fer	carry	transfer	_____
gener	bring forth	generation	_____
homo	same	homogenous	_____
ject	throw	rejection	_____
log	speak	monologue	_____
miss, mit	send	dismiss, transmit	_____
mur	wall	immure	_____
ocul	eye	ocular	_____
organ	system	organization	_____

Root	Definition	Example	Example
pater	father	paternity	_____
path	suffering, feeling	apathy	_____
pel	push	propel	_____
phobia	fear	acrophobia	_____
phon	sound	phonetic	_____
port	carry	transport	_____
pon, pos, posit	put, place	imposition	_____
primus	first	primogeniture	_____
psych	mind	psychology	_____
quir	ask	query	_____
scope	see	telescope	_____
sect	cut	dissect	_____
sequi	follow	subsequent	_____
somnia	sleep	insomnia	_____
soro	sister	sorority	_____
struct	build	construction	_____
tact	touch	tactile	_____
tain, tent	hold	maintain	_____
theo	god	theology	_____
therma	heat	thermometer	_____
tract	drag, pull	intractable	_____
veter	old	veteran	_____
vis	see	revise	_____

—From Susan Pongratz, Instructor's Manual for *The Effective Reader*. New York: Pearson Longman, 2004. Reprinted by permission of Pearson Education, Inc., Glenview, IL.

Prefixes

A prefix appears at the beginning of a word and changes the meaning of a word. In fact, *pre-* means *before.* For instance, consider the word *faithful,* which means *loyal.* If you add the prefix *un-,* however, you negate the word, or change its meaning to a negative word, which means *not faithful* or *not loyal.* If you arrange the prefixes into categories, it is easier to remember them. Consider the following examples.

Negative	Placement	Numbers	Time
un- (not)	*ab-* (away)	*uni-* (one)	*pre-* (before)
il- (not)	*circum-* (around)	*bi-* (two)	*post-* (after)
anti- (against)	*trans-* (across)	*tri-* (three)	*re-* (again)
mis- (wrong)	*inter-* (between)	*cent-* (hundred)	*retro-* (back)
mal- (bad)	*peri-* (around)	*multi-* (many)	*inter-* (during)

EXAMPLE When writing out the answer to the math problem, Jack accidentally **transposed** the numbers 34 to 43, and that one error caused additional **miscalculations**, so his final answer was **incorrect.**

Transpose means: _____

Miscalculation means: _____

Incorrect means: _____

EXPLANATION Since the prefix *trans-* means *across, to transpose* means *to move things across.* The prefix *mis-* means *wrong*, so that reversal of numbers caused Jack's calculations to be wrong, which then resulted in a final answer that was *in*correct or *not* accurate.

Note: Some prefixes have multiple meanings. For example, while *im-* means *not* in the word *imperfect,* the prefix *im-* in *impassioned* increases the value so the word means *very passionate* or *fervent.* Likewise, while *in-* means *not*, the word *invaluable* means *irreplaceable.* Something invaluable is so precious that its value cannot be measured.

EXERCISE **1** Prefixes

Study the following words and their definitions to determine the definition of each prefix.

1. telepathy: ability to communicate one's thoughts over a distance
telescope: instrument used to magnify distant objects
telephoto: camera lens used to photograph distant objects

_____ *Tele-* means
a. far; distant.
b. large.
c. small.
d. close; near.

2. retrospective: characterized by looking at the past
   retrograde: moving backward
   retroversion: a tilting backward

   _____ *Retro-* means
       a. beginning.   c. backward.
       b. front.   d. forward.

3. prognosis: doctor's opinion of a patient's anticipated medical outcome
   propel: push forward
   proponent: supporter of a particular idea or cause

   _____ *Pro-* means
       a. backward.   c. after.
       b. forward.   d. around.

4. autocrat: ruler with absolute power
   autonomy: independence
   automatic: done by itself, without conscious thought

   _____ *Auto-* means
       a. power.   c. self.
       b. group.   d. danger.

5. perennial: continuing through the years
   persevere: to continue in an undertaking in spite of difficulty
   persistent: continuing

   _____ *Per-* means
       a. through.   c. perfect.
       b. after.   d. long.

6. rerun: run again
   rehabilitate: bring again to a normal state of health
   revitalize: energize and bring again to a livelier state

   _____ *Re-* means
       a. under, below.   c. after.
       b. before.   d. again.

7. commemorate: to honor with others
   committee: a group that meets together
   commencement: an occasion for getting together to honor graduates

   _____ *Com-* means
       a. alone.   c. with; together.
       b. separate.   d. many.

8. ambidextrous: skilled with both hands
ambivalent: having mixed feelings
ambiguous: capable of being understood in two or more ways

_____ *Ambi-* means
    a. both.
    b. one.
    c. many.
    d. alone.

9. polygon: many-sided figure
monopolize: to assume complete control of a group or service
polyglot: one who speaks many languages

_____ *Poly-* means
    a. two.
    b. four.
    c. single.
    d. many.

10. metamorphosis: change of physical form
metaphysical: relating to something beyond that of the natural world
metaplasia: transforming of tissue to another form

_____ *Meta-* means
    a. beyond.
    b. first.
    c. simple.
    d. near.

EXERCISE 2 Prefixes

Study the chart below and insert a second example of a word that contains each prefix.

Prefixes Guide

Prefix	Definition	Example	Example
a-	not, without	apolitical	_____
ab-	away, from	absent	_____
auto-	self	autonomy	_____
bi-	two	bilingual	_____
circum-	around	circumspect	_____
con-	with, together	constitute	_____
de-	down, from, away	demoralize	_____
dis-	not, separated from	disinterest	_____
e-	out, from	evolve	_____
epi-	upon	epicenter	_____

Prefix	Definition	Example	Example
hyper-	above, excessive	hypertension	_____
hypo-	below, under	hypodermic	_____
im-	not	imperfect	_____
in-	not	incomprehensible	_____
ir-	not	irresponsible	_____
micro-	small	microscopic	_____
mono-	one	monopoly	_____
per-	through	perimeter	_____
pro-	forward, for	propel	_____
re-	again	replay	_____
retro-	backward	retroactive	_____
sub-	under, below	submarine	_____
super-	above, over, beyond	supervisor	_____
sus-	up from below	sustain	_____
sym-	together, with	symmetry	_____
tele-	far, from a distance	televise	_____

—From Susan Pongratz, Instructor's Manual for *The Effective Reader.* New York: Pearson Longman, 2004.
Reprinted by permission of Pearson Education, Inc., Glenview, IL.

Suffixes

A suffix appears at the end of a word and changes the meaning of a word as well as its part of speech. For instance, the base word *supervise* (verb) can be changed slightly by dropping the *e* and adding the suffix *-or* to create the word *supervisor* (noun) or *–ory* to create the word *supervisory* (adjective) or *-ion* to create the word *supervision* (noun).

EXAMPLE   The word *chronological*, which means *in time order,* comes from the root *chron* (order, time) added to the suffix *–ical* (like, related to). However, using the same root *chron*, you can also make 12 more words. Use your dictionary to identify the parts of speech and definitions for the following words.

1. anachronism: _____

_____

2. chronic: _____

3. chronicle: _____

_____

4. chronobiology: _____

5. chronogram: _____

6. chronograph: _____

7. chronologist: _____

8. chronology: _____

_____

9. chronometer: _____

10. chronotherapy: _____

11. synchronicity: _____

12. synchronize: _____

EXPLANATION Most of the suffixes added to the root *chron* indicate a noun: *–ism, –icle, –logy, –gram, –gist, –meter, –icity.* One of the verbs is indicated with the suffix *–ize,* and the only adjective ends with the suffix *–ic.*

EXERCISE **1** Suffixes

Study the following words and their definitions to determine the definition of each suffix.

1. capable: having the ability to do something
pliable: having the ability to bend
unflappable: not easily excited

_____ *-Able* means
a. not.
b. like.
c. capable of.
d. causing to become.

2. terminate: cause to end
alleviate: cause to become better; relieve
escalate: increase

_____ *-Ate* means
a. cause to become.
b. able to.
c. state or condition.
d. like.

3. destruction: state of tearing down
   promotion: act of advancing
   automation: act of using self-operating machinery

   _____ -*Tion* means
       a. resembling; like.   c. state; action.
       b. in a certain manner.   d. one who does.

4. critical: acting like a judge; serving as a decision point
   whimsical: characterized by light-heartedness
   comical: funny

   _____ -*Cal* means
       a. full of.   c. like; resembling.
       b. state; condition.   d. one who does.

5. synthesize: put parts into a whole
   summarize: to sum up
   tantalize: to tease

   _____ -*Ize* means
       a. state; condition.   c. full of.
       b. resembling.   d. make.

6. chemist: an expert in chemistry
   biologist: one who studies biology
   graphologist: handwriting expert

   _____ -*Ist* means
       a. expert.   c. like.
       b. full of.   d. state.

7. childish: like a child
   selfish: characterized by self-interest
   clownish: resembling a clown

   _____ -*Ish* means
       a. condition; state.   c. full of.
       b. make.   d. resembling.

8. author: one who writes
   doctor: physician
   actor: someone who plays roles on stage or in film

_____ -*Or* means
- a. state; condition.
- b. full of.
- c. characteristic of.
- d. one who.

9. preference: favorite
persistence: action involving determination
dependence: process involving trust

_____ -*Ence* means
- a. resembling.
- b. like; related to.
- c. state; quality.
- d. one who does something.

10. cleanliness: condition of being free from dirt or marks
fairness: equality
kindness: state of having compassion

_____ -*Ness* means
- a. one who does.
- b. quality; condition.
- c. process.
- d. cause to become.

EXERCISE **2** Suffixes

Study the chart below and insert a second example of a word that contains each suffix and note its part of speech.

Suffixes Guide

Suffix	Definition	Example	Example	Part of Speech
-able	capable of	portable	_____	_____
-acle	quality, state	spectacle	_____	_____
-al	of, like, related to	focal	_____	_____
-an	one who	vegetarian	_____	_____
-ate	make, cause to become	graduate	_____	_____
-ation	action, process	imitation	_____	_____
-er	person, doer	teacher	_____	_____
-ful	full of	beautiful	_____	_____
-ible	capable of	compatible	_____	_____
-ic	of, like, related to,	toxic	_____	_____

Suffix	Definition	Example	Example	Part of Speech
-ic	of, like, related to, being	toxic	_____	_____
-ical	of, like, related to	stoical	_____	_____
-ician	specialist	technician	_____	_____
-ify	cause to become	glorify	_____	_____
-ile	of, like, related to, being	infantile	_____	_____
-ist	person	chemist	_____	_____
-ition	action, process	nutrition	_____	_____
-ity	quality, trait	quantity	_____	_____
-ive	of, like, related to, being	sensitive	_____	_____
-ize	cause to become	tantalize	_____	_____
-less	without	penniless	_____	_____
-ly	in a certain manner	slowly	_____	_____
-ness	quality, state	cleanliness	_____	_____
-oid	like	humanoid	_____	_____
-ology	science, study of	microbiology	_____	_____
-or	person, doer	author	_____	_____
-ous	full of, like	loquacious	_____	_____
-tion	state, condition	matriculation	_____	_____
-y	quality, trait	showy	_____	_____

—From Susan Pongratz, Instructor's Manual for *The Effective Reader.* New York: Pearson Longman, 2004. Reprinted by permission of Pearson Education, Inc., Glenview, IL.

Analogies

Analogies are word relationships that require critical thinking. The pairs of words are like puzzles that require the reader to determine the relationship presented. For example, daughter : girl :: son : boy. You would read this analogy as, "Daughter is to girl as son is to boy." Note that the first step is to make sure you know the definitions of all of the words. Next, you determine the relationship presented.

Analogies can present several kinds of relationships.

- Synonym (kind : nice :: unfriendly : mean).
- Antonym (friendly : mean :: heavy : light).
- A descriptive relationship (strong : wrestler :: tall : skyscraper).
- The relationship of the part to a whole (leg : body :: tire : car).
- The relationship of an item to a category (cabin : dwelling :: painting : art).

EXERCISE 1 Synonyms and Antonyms

Step 1: Determine the definitions and part of speech of each of the pairs presented.
Step 2: Determine the relationship of the first pair.
Step 3: Select the letter of the answer that completes the second pair with the same relationship as the first pair.

1. rug : carpet :: curtain : _____
   a. drape   b. cover   c. pillow

2. start : beginning :: end : _____
   a. center   b. avoid   c. finish

3. disappoint : please :: anticipate : _____
   a. relive   b. forget   c. expect

4. courageous : afraid :: brave : _____
   a. cowardly   b. sensitive   c. thoughtful

5. exhaust : energize :: dirty : _____
   a. clean   b. filthy   c. creative

6. active : dormant :: busy : _____
   a. expensive   b. overbooked   c. available

7. deceptive : honest :: grieving : _____
   a. musical   b. joyous   c. sad

8. outrageous : predictable :: easygoing : _____
   a. severe   b. strict   c. alone

9. efficient : careless :: bored : _____
   a. fed up   b. interested   c. tired

10. healthy : ill :: serious : _____
    a. silly   b. humorless   c. afraid

EXERCISE **2** Descriptive, Part to Whole, Item to Category

1. price : tax :: bridge : _____
  a. toll   b. span   c. water

2. disease : bird flu :: jet : _____
  a. ship   b. Mustang   c. Boeing 767

3. island : Puerto Rico :: mountain : _____
  a. Empire State Building   b. South Padre   c. Mt. Everest

4. food : flavorful :: thief : _____
  a. dull   b. dishonest   c. honest

5. running back : fast :: ballerina : _____
  a. slow   b. fat   c. graceful

6. sports car : Corvette :: truck : _____
  a. VW Jetta   b. Ford F-150   c. Ford Mustang

7. protection : sunscreen :: shine : _____
  a. sun block   b. polish   c. burn

8. shout : loud :: murmur : _____
  a. simple   b. soft   c. silent

9. sky : expansive :: ocean : _____
  a. narrow   b. small   c. vast

10. inventory : list :: team roster : _____
  a. announce   b. erase   c. ignore

Stop and Think

 Read the following passage from a college psychology textbook and use context clues to select the best word from the box to fill in the blanks.

distance   eyes   interactions   patients   people

To explain the concept of personal space in the United States, anthropologist Edward Hall classified four spatial zones, or distances, used in social interactions with other people: the intimate, the personal, the social, and the public. An *intimate distance* (from zero to 18 inches) is maintained between two **(1)** _____ who have great familiarity with one another. It is an acceptable **(2)** _____ for comforting someone who is hurt or for **(3)** _____ between lovers, physicians and **(4)** _____, and athletes. The closeness enables someone to hold another person, look into the other's **(5)** _____, and hear the other's breath. An acceptable distance between friends and acquaintances is *personal space* (1.5 to 4 feet); this is the distance for most social interactions. *Social distance* (4 to 12 feet) is used for business and most interactions with strangers. At 4 to 6 feet, people are close enough to communicate their ideas effectively but far enough away to remain separated. *Public distance* (12 to 25 feet or more) minimizes personal contact. It is the distance maintained between politicians and audiences, teachers and students, and actors or musicians and their audience.

—From Lester A. Lefton and Linda Brannon, *Psychology,* 8e, pp. 635-636. Published by Allyn and Bacon, Boston, MA. Copyright © 2003 by Pearson Education. Reprinted by permission of the publisher.

 Visit the following Websites for more practice with context clues and word parts.

http://wps.ablongman.com/long_licklider_vocabulary_1/0,1682, 11668-,00.html

http://wps.ablongman.com/long_licklider_vocabulary_1/0,1682, 11839-,00.html

CHAPTER 2

Using a Dictionary Effectively

Get Ready to Read About Dictionary Applications

A good collegiate dictionary and a thesaurus are important tools for a college student. Learning to use all of the features of a dictionary enhances your communication skills—both oral and written. As you prepare to read this chapter, think about what you already know about the type of the information a dictionary, a thesaurus, and a book glossary provide. Also, think about ways you can use these tools when preparing for classes and writing research papers.

Linguists are people who study language. They consider the origins of words as well as how language changes because it is dynamic and constantly evolving. For example, you are familiar with the word *lifestyle*, which means *a way of life.* This word first appeared in 1929, and it finally became an accepted part of the American vocabulary in the early 1960s. Some words are created and added to dictionaries each year based on the frequency with which they are used. For example, recent additions to the new edition of *Merriam-Webster Collegiate Dictionary* include *mouse potatoes* (people who spend a lot of time in front of the computer), *himbo* (a handsome, superficial man), and *polyamory* (the practice of having more than one romantic relationship at a time). Likewise, as they become outdated, words are eliminated or labeled *archaic* or *obsolete,* which means they are no longer in use. A treasure chest of information, a current collegiate dictionary is an essential tool for every college student.

Consider the following features of most dictionaries:

- Guide Words (the words at the top of each page)
- Spelling (how the word and its different forms are spelled)
- Syllabication (the word divided into syllables)
- Pronunciation (how to say the word)
- Part of speech (the type of word)
- Definition (the meaning of the word, with the most common meaning listed first)
- Synonyms (words that have similar meaning)
- Etymology (the history of the word)

How to Find and Read Word Entries in the Dictionary

Spelling and Syllables

The spelling of the word is first given in bold type. In addition, the word is divided into syllables. A syllable is a unit of sound, and it includes one vowel sound. For instance, the word *read* has two vowels, *e* and *a,* but only one vowel sound, which is a long *e.*

In words with more than one syllable, the stress marks that indicate the syllables that are emphasized will guide you in the proper pronunciation of the word.

Note: Often, adding a suffix can change the stress and thus the pronunciation of a word.

EXAMPLE *prefer* (prĭ-fûr′)   *preferable* (prĕf′ər-ə-bəl)

EXPLANATION *Prefer* has two syllables. The second syllable is stressed more than the first, which is apparent because of the primary stress mark after the letter *r.* Now note how the stress mark changes for the word *preferable,* which has four syllables. The first syllable is now the one that is stressed more than the other three syllables. As you can see, learning to read the symbols in a dictionary entry will help you communicate more effectively, and noting the stress marks is critical to pronouncing words correctly. For this reason, dictionaries contain a pronunciation key.

Pronunciation Symbols

Study the chart below to learn how to interpret other symbols when using a dictionary for pronunciation.

Syllable	A unit of sound that includes at least one vowel sound.
Brève ⌣	This indicates a short vowel sound: ă = mat ŏ = hot ĕ = den ŭ = cup ĭ = sit
Macron —	This indicates a long vowel sound, which "says" the name of the letter. For example: ā (dā = day) ē (sē = see) ī (hīd = hide) ō (grō = grow) yōō (kyōōt = cute)
Schwa ə	This indicates the vowel sound of an unaccented syllable and is always pronounced "uh." ago item festival famous gypsum ə-gō′ ī′-təm fĕs′-tə-v'l fā′-məs jĭp′-səm

EXERCISE 1 Pronunciation Symbols

Apply your understanding of phonetic symbols to decode the following quotations.

1. "drēmz kŭm trōō; wǐ*th*-out′ *th*ăt pŏs′ə-bǐl′ǐ-tē, nā′chər wŏŏd nŏt ǐn-sǐt′ ŭs tōō hăv *th*ĕm."—John Updike

_____

_____

2. "ĕv′rē tīm yōō wāk ŭp ənd ăsk yoŏr-sĕlf′, 'hwŏt goŏd thǐngz ăm ī gō′ǐng tōō dōō tə-dā′?', rǐ-mĕm′bər *th*ăt hwĕn *th*ə sŭn gōz doun ăt sŭn′sĕt′, ǐt wǐl tāk ə pärt ŭv yoŏr līf wǐ*th* ǐt."—Indian proverb

_____

_____

_____

3. "dō nŏt dwĕl ǐn *th*ə păst, dō nŏt drēm ŭv *th*ə fyōōchər, kŏn′sən-trāt′ *th*ə mīnd ŏn *th*ə prĕz′ənt mō′mənt."—Buddha

_____

_____

4. "ǐf yōō dōn't hăv *th*ə tīm tōō rēd, yōō dōnt hăv *th*ə tīm ôr *th*ə tōōlz tōō rīt."—Stephen King

_____

_____

Study the dictionary entry below.

run-ner \′rə-nər \ n (14c) **1a :** one that runs: RACER **b :** BASE RUNNER **c :** BALL-CARRIER **2a :** MESSENGER **b :** one that smuggles or distributes illicit or contra-band goods (as drugs, liquor, or guns) **3 :** any of several large vigorous carangid fishes **4a :** either of the longitudinal pieces on which a sled or sleigh slides **b :** the part of a skate that slides on the ice : BLADE **c :** the support of a drawer or a sliding door **5a :** an elongated horizontal stem arising from the base of a plant: *esp:* STOLON 1a **b :** a plant (as a strawberry) that forms or spreads by means of runners **c :** a twining vine (as a scarlet runner bean) **6a :** a long nar-row carpet for a hall or staircase **b :** a narrow decorative cloth cover for a table or dresser top **7 :** an adjustable backstay running from mast to rail on a sail boat or ship **8 :** a running shot in basketball

—By permission. From *Merriam-Webster's Collegiate® Dictionary, Eleventh Edition*
© 2003 by Merriam-Webster Inc. (http://www.merriam-webster.com).

Definitions

Dictionary entries usually have more than one meaning, so the definitions will be numbered, followed by the part of speech. The definition will sometimes be accompanied by a sentence of explanation of usage to clarify each meaning.

Multiple Meanings and Context Clues

To determine which of the multiple meanings you should use, apply what you have learned about context clues. Knowing how to recognize the parts of speech will also be a guide to the appropriate definition.

EXAMPLE   Study the dictionary excerpt for *runner,* then select the number of the definition that best fits its use in the sentences below.

_____   **1.** We purchased a new Oriental-style runner for the staircase.

_____   **2.** He was a charming man, but we later learned he was a guns runner during the war.

_____   **3.** The runner was a surprise goal, and our basketball team won by a margin.

EXPLANATION

1. The rug on the staircase corresponds to the definition "a long narrow carpet for a hall or staircase."

2. A smuggler runs guns and liquor.

3. The word "basketball" is the clue to determine definition 8.

Connotation and Denotation

To communicate effectively, you will recognize that many words have a denotation as well as a connotation. **Denotation** means the dictionary definition. **Connotation** means the implied, or suggested, meaning. Furthermore, some words may have a positive connotation or a negative connotation. Think about the words *lie* and *embellish.* Although both can mean stretching the truth, *to lie* sounds much more evil than *to embellish the truth.*

Marketing strategies often involve recognizing the power of language. For example, because of the positive connotation of *cottage,* you would use that term, rather than *small house* if you were a realtor because the first term sounds charming while the second sounds cramped. Likewise, as a jeweler, you might market a delicately styled diamond rather than a small one. The first description focuses on something dainty and refined, while a small diamond might imply tiny and cheap.

EXAMPLE

Check the statement below that has a positive connotation.

_____ He is one of the most eccentric writers I know.

_____ He is one of the weirdest writers I know.

_____ He is one of the most idiotic writers I know.

EXPLANATION   Although you would not say anything as negative as, "He is one of the most idiotic writers I know," many people prefer *eccentric* because it suggests an interesting person, while *idiotic* sounds negative and judgmental.

EXERCISE **2** Connotation

Insert the letter of the wording with the more positive connotation.

1. In a speech praising Delegate Oder, Ben said, "He is a true _____."
   a. politician   b. statesman

2. When caught with the merchandise he had not paid for, the man said, "I have done nothing wrong because these things are only _____."
   a. stolen   b. liberated

3. Although the child became increasingly more difficult to handle, his mother defended him saying, "He isn't bad; he's only _____."
   a. pig-headed   b. strong-willed

Etymology

Dictionary entries often begin with a history, or etymology, of the word. This information reveals the origin of the word and its meaning as well as how the word's connotation may have changed.

Sometimes the etymology involves word parts such as a prefix, root, or suffix. For other words, the etymology is connected to stories that provide a framework for the word. Often, knowing the story helps you remember the definition of the word. Study the following example from Greek mythology.

ODYSSEY

The word *odyssey* comes from the Greek myth about Odysseus, the Greek hero in *The Odyssey* by Homer. The king of Ithaca, Odysseus went to the Trojan War and then took ten years to return home. During that decade, he experienced many adventures. Today when a person is on a long journey, especially to achieve a goal, we say he or she is on an odyssey.

Like Odysseus who took many years to return home, a college student is on an **odyssey** to earn a degree.

Molly Gamble-Walker

Dictionary Skills Review

Read the following story, and underline each time you see the word *draft* appear in the passage.

THE MYSTERIOUS LEGACY

Dear Board Members:

I sit here writing the final draft of my last letter to you as the president and chief executive officer of Cline Energy Resources. While I take a draft of my tea and enjoy a nearby fire to endure the ever-present draft from the winter storm, I take heart in knowing I will soon retire to my yacht on the warm coast of the Gulf.

For additional entertainment, I have prepared a game, so that you can discover which of you will be promoted to take my place. To do this, however, you must first determine the combination to the safe behind the painting in the boardroom. Then you will learn the name of your new leader as well as the amount of the generous bonuses I have allotted for the rest of you.

But first, let me reminisce.

I started this company from the money I saved after I returned from the war. When I received my draft notice at 18, I had no idea the adventures ahead. In the army, I learned the skills of discipline and leadership and the importance of identifying champions and developing allies. I also learned how to cast a net and then haul in a draft of fish my men and I could savor. (Always take time to show how you value others, and they will work harder for you and the cause.) I'll never forget that time the boat was so heavy with our catch that the draft was at least two feet deeper in the water. Ah, yes! I learned survival skills that have helped me in the corporate world.

All of that was a long time ago.

And now it is time to solve the puzzle. Like a stone cutter's draft used to keep things level, I am asking you to think clearly and cleverly to determine your next leader. Trust him. Be a champion for him. Align yourself with him. Help him develop loyal allies as well. Be a strong team and Cline Energy Resources will continue to grow with integrity.

My best to you all,
Franklin O'Neal Keller

You Are the Detective

To determine the combination of the safe, the board members first identified the number of the dictionary definition that corresponded to each context of the word *draft*.

draft (drăft, draft) n. **1. a.** A current of air in an enclosed area. **b.** A device in a flue controlling the circulation of air. **2. a.** A pull or traction of a load. **b.** Something that is pulled or drawn. **c.** A team of animals used to pull or draw a load. **3.** The depth of a vessel's keel below the water line, esp. when loaded. **4.** A heavy demand upon resources. **5.** A documentary instrument for transferring money. **6. a.** A gulp, swallow, or inhalation. **b.** The amount taken in by a single act of drinking or inhaling. **c.** A measured portion; dose. **7. a.** The drawing of a liquid, as from a cask or keg. **b.** The amount drawn. **8. a.** A selection of one or more individuals from a group for a particular purpose or duty: the convention drafted a candidate. **b.** Conscription for military service **c.** The body of a people selected or conscripted. **d.** *Sports.* A system in which professional teams get the exclusive rights to new players. **9. a.** The act of drawing in a fishnet. **b.** The catch. **10. a.** A preliminary outline of a plan, document, or picture: *the first draft of a report.* **b.** a representation of something to be constructed. **11.** A narrow line chiseled on a stone to guide the stonecutter in leveling its surface. **12.** A slight taper given a die to facilitate the removal of casting. v. draft-ed, draft-ing, drafts-tr.

—Adapted from *Webster's New World Dictionary, Second College Edition,* ed. David B. Guralnik, p. 423. Copyright © 1970 by Simon & Schuster, Inc. Reprinted with permission of John Wiley & Sons, Inc.

Step 1: Underline the word *draft* and determine the context that corresponds to the definitions in the dictionary excerpt.

Step 2: Write the number of each definition that corresponds to the context in the letter.

_____ - _____ - _____ - _____ - _____ - _____ - _____

Stop and Think

 Go to **www.merriamwebster.com** and **www.etymonline.com** to view online resources for the word *amplify*, then answer the following:

1. Which one provides the phonetic spelling of a word? _____

2. Which one provides the part of speech for the word? _____

3. Which one provides synonyms? _____

4. Which one provides antonyms? _____

   _____

5. Which one provides the history of the word? _____

 Go to **www.wiktionary.org** and determine what features are provided in a variety of languages.

_____

_____

Review Test
Chapters 1 and 2

1 Word Parts

Match the definitions in Column 2 to the word parts in Column 1.

Column 1		Column 2
_____	**1.** inter-	a. far
_____	**2.** ambi-	b. please
_____	**3.** dis-	c. with; together
_____	**4.** re-	d. through
_____	**5.** –tion	e. time
_____	**6.** –ize	f. for; forward
_____	**7.** auto-	g. between
_____	**8.** di-	h. city
_____	**9.** graph-	i. back; backward
_____	**10.** vis	j. move
_____	**11.** poli	k. both
_____	**12.** fluct, flux	l. again
_____	**13.** grat	m. self
_____	**14.** cede	n. state; condition
_____	**15.** retro-	o. two
_____	**16.** tele-	p. not; separated from

_____ **17.** pro-   q. make; cause to become

_____ **18.** per-   r. flow

_____ **19.** com-   s. see

_____ **20.** chron   t. write; draw

2 Context Clues

Using context clues, select the letter of the best definition of the word in **bold** print.

_____ **1.** Mike agreed to serve as the committee chair for the next **biennium**, so we knew his schedule would be full for the next two years.
   a. month   c. two years
   b. year   d. five years

_____ **2.** Soaring gasoline prices **prompted** Stacy to trade in her SUV for a more fuel-efficient vehicle.
   a. encouraged   c. bothered
   b. discouraged   d. surprised

_____ **3.** Even though he was **averse** to hard work, Jay decided to save money and single-handedly tackle the job of painting the outside of his house.
   a. difficult   c. enthusiastic
   b. inclined   d. opposed

_____ **4.** Our supervisor's instructions were too **vague**, so several co-workers agreed to send someone to his office to get directions that were more clearly stated.
   a. clear   c. promising
   b. unclear   d. unsure

_____ **5.** In moments of **duress**, such as driving in heavy traffic or working to complete a project with a nearly impossible deadline, George remains calm and shows no signs of stress.
   a. persuasion   c. pressure
   b. permission   d. calm

_____ **6.** The interview candidate seemed **unflappable** as he answered the company president's questions with ease, never appearing nervous or tense.
a. composed
b. worried
c. concerned
d. restless

_____ **7.** We searched for a **pragmatic** solution—not something impractical and impossible to use.
a. idealistic
b. romantic
c. nervous
d. practical

_____ **8.** Anyone can get a "big hair" look with this new shampoo because it will make your locks more **voluminous**.
a. small
b. polite
c. full
d. flat

_____ **9.** We wondered why the couple needed such a **commodious** house—especially when they did not have much furniture to fill it.
a. small
b. spacious
c. crowded
d. well-built

_____ **10.** Although most people need **tangible** rewards such as a bonus check, extra vacation time, or a promotion, some only desire a feeling of personal satisfaction for having done a good job.
a. free
b. concrete; visible
c. difficult to find
d. unpopular

3 Context Clues and Word Parts

Step 1: Identify the type of context clue presented in the sentence and underline the word(s) you used to determine the definition of the word in **bold** print; then write the definition of the word part(s).
Step 2: Select the letter of the definition of the word.

1. If you agree to allow your boat to be used by the Coast Guard Auxiliary in time of war, then you can **circumvent** paying personal property taxes on it, and that savings is often a great deal of money.

Context Clue: _____

Word Parts: *circum-*: _____; *ven*: _____

_____ **Circumvent** means
a. surround.
b. avoid.
c. ensure.
d. agree.

2. **Archaic** words that are no longer used, such as *receipt* for *recipe*, can confuse students who are learning English.

Context Clue: _____

Word Parts: *arch* _____; *-ic* : _____

_____ **Archaic** means
   a. out of date.   c. popular.
   b. modern.   d. easy to remember.

3. We stood at the edge of the mountain to get a good view, but suddenly experienced **acrophobia;** our fear made us carefully move back.

Context Clue: _____

Word Parts: *acro-* : _____; *phobia*: _____

_____ **Acrophobia** means
   a. fear of mountains.   c. fear of wild animals.
   b. fear of boredom.   d. fear of heights.

4. In **retrospect,** Wayne should have spent more time researching the area before he agreed to accept the job and relocate.

Context Clue: _____

Word Parts: *retro-* _____; *spect*: _____

_____ **Retrospect** means
   a. new view.   c. a careless study.
   b. looking back again.   d. backward thinking.

5. Many Greeks were **polytheists**, honoring Olympian gods such as Zeus, Hera, Apollo, and Athena.

Context Clue: _____

Word Parts: *poly-* _____; *theo*: god; *-ist*: _____

_____ **Polytheist** means
   a. history of religion.
   b. one who believes in imaginary things.
   c. one who believes in many gods.
   d. absolute ruler.

6. He was a true statesman, someone who always sought an **equitable** compromise, instead of insisting on a selfish decision.

Context Clue: _____

Word Parts: *equ:* _____; *-able:* _____

_____ **Equitable** means
- a. difficult.
- b. fair.
- c. meaningless.
- d. unfair.

7. As a young man, Jon was playful and irresponsible, with no fatherly qualities until he finally married, and became the father of a son; since then, he has become one of the most **paternal** men I have ever known.

Context Clue: _____

Word Parts: *pater:* _____; *-al:* _____

_____ **Paternal** means
- a. fatherly.
- b. motherly.
- c. playful.
- d. not responsible.

8. Our reunions are **multigenerational**, so young children have a chance to hear many stories from the older family members.

Context Clue: _____

Word Parts: *multi:* _____; *gen:* _____; *-tion:*

_____; *-al:* _____

_____ **Multigenerational** means
- a. characterized by one generation.
- b. characterized by people of many ages.
- c. characterized by elderly people.
- d. many young people.

9. If you **inject** the stem of a white carnation with food coloring, you can change the color of the blossom.

Context Clue: _____

Word Parts: *in-:* _____; *ject:* _____

_____ *Inject* means
- a. find.
- b. insert.
- c. ignore.
- d. cut.

1

10. To avoid getting **hypothermia,** you will need to wear a wet suit for winter surfing.

Context Clue: _____

Word Parts: *hypo-:* _____; *therm-* _____

_____ *Hypothermia* means
   a. condition of below-normal body temperature.
   b. condition of above-normal body temperature.
   c. bruising from constant impact.
   d. fever.

4 Phonetic Analysis

Write out the quotations that are spelled phonetically here.

1. "hwŏt wē sē dĭ-pĕndz′ mān′lē ŏn hwŏt wē lo͞ok fôr."—John Lubbock

_____

2. "*thə* spĭr′ĭt ŭv rī-zĭs′təns to͞o gŭv′ərn-mənt ĭz sō văl-yo͞o′ə-b'l ŏn sûr′tn ə-kā′zhənz, *thăt* ī wĭsh ĭt ôl′wāz to͞o bē kĕpt ə-līv."—Thomas Jefferson

_____

_____

3. "*thə* sē′krĭt ŭv joi ĭn work ĭz kən-tānd′ ĭn wŭn wûrd—ĕk′sə-ləns. to͞o nō hou to͞o do͞o sŭm′thĭng wĕl ĭz to͞o ĕn-joi′ ĭt."—Pearl S. Buck

_____

_____

4. "wē är hwŏt wē rĭ-pē′tĭd-lē do͞o. ĕk′sə-ləns *thĕn* ĭz nŏt ən ăkt, bŭt ə hăb′ĭt."—Aristotle

_____

_____

5. "ôl′wāz ăk-nŏl′ĭj ə fôlt. *thĭs* wĭl thrō *thōz* ĭn ə-thôr′ĭ-tə ôf *thăr* gärd ənd gĭv yo͞o ən ŏp′ər-to͞o nĭ-tē to͞o kə-mĭt′ môr." —Mark Twain

_____

_____

5 Dictionary Usage

Use your dictionary to answer the following questions.*

1. What is the first definition of the word *spirit*? _____

_____

2. What is the part of speech of the French term *en masse*? _____

3. How many definitions are listed for the word *fat*? _____

4. How many syllables in the word *exasperate*? _____

5. What does *exasperate* mean? _____

6. What is a synonym for *exasperate*? _____

7. What year did the word *exasperate* appear? _____

8. What is the obsolete definition of *exasperate*? _____

9. What two parts of speech can the word *melt* serve? _____

10. What is one example presented of a sentence using the verb *melted*?

_____

*Suggested answers are based on *Merriam-Webster's Collegiate Dictionary*, 11th ed.

CHAPTER

3

Vocabulary and Physical Health

Get Ready to Read About Physical Health

College health textbooks contain reading selections on a variety of subjects related to physical, mental, and emotional well-being. In addition, you will encounter chapters about the environment as well as those dealing with physical and mental stress. In this selection, you will read about a problem of great concern on many college campuses: binge drinking. The word *binge* means *unrestrained* and *excessive*. Before you read, consider what you already know about the following word parts. The meanings of some have been provided. Recall what you learned in Chapter 1 and fill in the blanks for the others.

1. The prefix *com-* means *with, together*.

2. The prefix *de-* means _____.

3. The prefix *ob-* means *to*.

4. The prefix *pre-* means _____.

5. The root *via* means *way*.

6. The suffix *-ate* means _____ and indicates a _____.

7. The suffix *-ence* means _____ and indicates a _____.

8. The suffix *-ness* means *quality, state, condition* and indicates a

   _____.

9. The suffix *-ous* means *like, full of, related to* and indicates an

   _____.

10. The suffix *-tion* means *action, state* and indicates a _____.

---

compulsiveness	deprive	deviant	obtain	prevalence
denigrate	despite	grave	perilous	ramification

BINGE DRINKING

Despite laws in every state that make it illegal for anyone under the age of 21 to purchase or possess alcohol, young people report that alcohol is easy to **obtain** and that many high school and college students drink with one goal in mind—to get drunk. Binge drinking is defined as consuming five or more drinks in a row for boys and four or more in a row for girls. The alarming aspects of binge drinking cannot be overlooked or underestimated.

One troubling aspect of binge drinking is its **prevalence** among youth and college students. Often starting as young as age 13, these drinkers tend to increase bingeing during adolescence. The behavior peaks in young adulthood, which includes the ages from 18 to 22. Then this **perilous** conduct slowly decreases. According to a 1997 national study, among 12- to 20-year-olds, 15 percent were binge drinkers. A 1995 study found that nearly half of all college students surveyed drank four or five drinks in one sitting within a two-week period. In addition, students who live in fraternity and sorority houses are the heaviest drinkers. Over 80 percent of them reported that they take part in binge drinking.

Binge drinking is risky behavior that has serious **ramifications.** The **gravest** effect is alcohol poisoning, which is an acute physical reaction to an overdose of the drug. During bingeing, the brain is **deprived** of oxygen. This lack of oxygen eventually causes the brain to shut down the heart and lungs.

Alcohol poisoning has several symptoms. They include vomiting and uncon-sciousness. In addition, the skin becomes cold, clammy, pale or bluish in color. Breathing becomes slow or irregular.

Binge drinking brings about other disturbing behaviors or effects as well. In schools with high binge drinking rates, binge drinkers are likely to in-sult, **denigrate**, push, or hit their peers. Frequent binge drinkers were eight times more likely than nonbinge drinkers to miss a class, fall behind in schoolwork, get hurt or injured, and damage property. Binge drinking during college may be linked to mental health disorders. These disorders include **compulsiveness**, depression or anxiety, or early **deviant** behavior. Alarmingly, nearly one out of every five teenagers has experienced "blackout" spells. During these spells, they could not remember what happened the pre-vious evening because of heavy binge drinking. Finally, many who are fre-quent binge drinkers also drink and drive.

–From D. J. Henry, *The Effective Reader*, Updated Edition. Pearson Longman, 2004.
Reprinted by permission of Pearson Education, Inc., Glenview, IL.
Adapted from U.S. Department of Health and Human Services,
"Binge Drinking in Adolescents and College Students."

VISUAL VOCABULARY

Rock climbing can be fun if you take some precautions in

_____ areas.

a. deviant
b. perilous

Elizabeth Pongratz

EXERCISE 1 Context Clues

Refer to the previous passage and use context clues from the sentences below to determine the definition of each of the following words in **bold** print. Do not consult a dictionary.

1. compulsiveness (kəm-pŭl′sĭv-něs)
   Psychologists recognize many kinds of love, but the manic lover is characterized by extreme highs and lows, possessiveness, and **compulsiveness,** so that the voices of jealousy and power are more important than compassion or caring for the other person.

   _____ **Compulsiveness** means
   a. higher power.
   b. extreme compassion.
   c. kindness and caring.
   d. the tendency to be driven by an outside force.

2. denigrate (děn′ĭ-grāt′) v.
   When the Olympic athlete **denigrated** the rest of his team, many fans were disappointed that he would criticize the very people he had trained with in hopes of a victory.

   _____ **Denigrate** means
   a. praise.   c. satisfy.
   b. belittle.   d. study.

3. deprive (dĭ-prīv′) v.
   When parents **deprive** a child of basic needs such as food, shelter, comfort, safety, and love, they tend to be either fearful or angry.

   _____ **Deprive** means
   a. provide.   c. share.
   b. take away.   d. serve.

4. despite (dĭ-spīt′) conj.
   Despite the grim weather forecast, which indicated heavy rain all week, we decided to take our chances and vacation at the beach.

   _____ **Despite** means
   a. regardless of.   c. because.
   b. finally.   d. as a result.

5. deviant (dē′vē-ənt) adj.
In our sociology class, we learned that some cultures praise activities we would label as **deviant** behavior because they admire the individuality and the courage of the participants and their willingness to stand out in a crowd.

_____ **Deviant** means
- a. quiet.
- b. abnormal.
- c. normal.
- d. average.

6. grave (grāv) adj.
When serving on jury duty, the jurors are reminded of the **grave** responsibility they have in coming to a decision in a murder trial.

_____ **Grave** means
- a. normal.
- b. serious.
- c. surprise.
- d. understanding.

7. obtain (əb-tān′) v.
Before I could drive in Europe, I had to **obtain** an international driver's license in order to rent a car.

_____ **Obtain** means
- a. rent.
- b. give.
- c. get.
- d. deliver.

8. perilous (pĕr′ə-ləs) adj.
When Indiana Jones clutches his heart just before crossing the gorge in search of the Holy Grail, all viewers share the terrifying moment, aware of his **perilous** situation.

_____ **Perilous** means
- a. dangerous.
- b. easy.
- c. famous.
- d. safe.

9. prevalence (′pre-və-lən(t)s) adj.
In architecture, there is a **prevalence** of arches in buildings such as the Eiffel Tower, Hoover Dam, and many Roman structures.

_____ **prevalence** means
- a. locality.
- b. discovery.
- c. lack.
- d. abundance.

10. ramification (răm′ə-fĭ-kā′shən) n.
    The **ramification** of a lie is often the need to tell another lie to cover up the first one, which then leads to another lie to cover up the one before that.

    _____ **Ramification** means
    a. cause.   c. exit.
    b. consequence.   d. beginning.

EXERCISE 2 Word Sorts

Synonyms
Match the word to the synonyms or definitions that follow each blank.

1. _____ acquire; get; achieve; secure

2. _____ dangerous; hazardous; risky; treacherous

3. _____ serious; sad; somber; gloomy

4. _____ belittle; defame; disparage; vilify

5. _____ consequence; effect; development; reaction

Antonyms
Select the letter of the word(s) with the opposite meaning.

_____ 6. compulsiveness
    a. extreme focus   c. earnestness
    b. flexibility   d. obsession

_____ 7. prevalence
    a. rarity   c. frequency
    b. abundance   d. regularity

_____ 8. despite
    a. even though   c. albeit
    b. in spite of   d. because

_____ 9. deviant
    a. abnormal   c. normal
    b. unusual   d. rare

_____ 10. deprive
    a. forgive   c. take away
    b. expect   d. provide

EXERCISE 3 Fill in the Blank

Use context clues to determine the word that best completes each sentence.

1. _____ his impressive intelligence, Dr. Webb acts like the typical absent-minded professor, never quite aware of his surroundings or the people in his presence, but always focused on his subject.

2. It is said that Mr. Sanders exhibits _____ over his landscape because he trims the grass with scissors and nail clippers.

3. Our situation became _____ when the bridge we had just crossed suddenly collapsed and we realized there was no way back across the dangerous gorge.

4. My brother tried a science experiment in which he _____ one plant of natural sunlight for several hours during the day, and he gave the other plant plenty of sun.

5. Patrons who _____ restaurant employees tend to be unkind to their coworkers.

6. At Halloween, people dress up like werewolves, vampires, ghouls, and other _____ characters.

7. The math professor wore a _____ expression as he prepared to return the corrected tests, and the room suddenly seemed full of gloom.

8. In the United States, comedians and cartoonists make fun of politicians without _____; however, in other countries there are often negative consequences when something uncomplimentary is said about a public official.

9. The _____ of computers has made some aspects of our lives more efficient, but it has also complicated other areas and forced us to keep up with the ever-changing technology.

10. "To _____ a boarding pass, you must go to the next available kiosk for self check-in and follow the instructions on the monitor," announced the airline representative.

EXERCISE **4** Application

Using context clues, insert the vocabulary word in the appropriate blank. A part-of-speech clue is given for each vocabulary word.

Keith smiled at his longtime high school friends who had gathered at the airport to see him off on his journey to Jalalabad, Afghanistan. This trip was not a result of a **(1)** (n.) _____ on his part. No, in fact, he had spent long hours researching the job opportunity, recognizing its **(2)** (adj.) _____ nature. While danger was possible, there would also be good work helping local farmers grow and export the harvest of a local orchard.

The job involved project managing, so he would organize the staff, plan the budget, and oversee the production of the apricots and almonds, thus helping the farmers **(3)** (v.) _____ some financial independence. The **(4)** (n.) _____ of illegal military action by the country's warlords and the financing of their efforts through the growth of the poppies used to make heroin added to his concern. **(5)** (conj.) _____ these dangers, there was a chance to improve the living conditions of people in this middle Eastern desert. Helping others to become hopeful about their future was also appealing. Still, the **(6)** (n.) _____of intruding on the illegal activity of **(7)** (adj.) _____ military leaders played on his mind.

How could he **(8)** (v.) _____ *these honest, good people of their chance for a better life?* he wondered.

Keith smiled at his friends Chris and Charlie who had driven him to the airport to show their support. They tried to hide their **(9)** (adj.) _____ expressions with jokes that seemed to

(10) (v.) _____ the job he had signed on to do. "Check out the job opportunities and we'll join you," Chris said. "Or we can open an import business—carpets and lapis!"

And then there was silence and long hugs. Good friends and adventure. *What could be better?* he thought as he turned to move through security and leave his friends behind.

Stop and Think

 Using a dictionary or **www.dictionary.com**, insert a form of the word. Note that some forms may not be applicable.

Noun	Verb	Adjective
compulsiveness		1._____
2._____	denigrate	
3._____	deprive	
4._____		deviant
prevalence		5._____
6._____	7._____	perilous

 Go to the following website to study the graph and then write a summary using three words from this chapter.

http://www.uscupstate.edu/campus_life/student_dev/drug/files/ gpa.pdf#search=%22drinks%20per%20week%20and%20gpa%22

_____

_____

_____

Vocabulary and Mental Health

Get Ready to Read About Mental Health

The following selection is from a general health textbook that covers topics about the physical and mental health as well as the emotional well-being of a person. Consider all you have heard and read about the mind–body connection. Think also of the effects stress has on a person mentally and physically. You are going to read about an addiction, which is an overdependence on something. In this case, however, it is not substance abuse that is the cause of the addiction; rather, it is work.

Before you read, consider what you already know about the following word parts. The meanings of some have been provided. Recall what you learned in Chapter 1 and fill in the blanks for the others.

1. The prefix *ob-* means _____.

2. The prefix *per-* means _____.

3. The prefix *peri-* means *around*.

4. The prefix *re-* means _____.

5. The root *grat* means *pleasing*.

6. The root *persona* means *person*.

7. The suffix *-ate* means *cause to become, make* and usually indicates

    a _____.

8. The suffix *-fy* means _____ and indicates a _____.

9. The suffix *-ion* means *act of* and indicates a _____.

10. The suffix *-ment* means *act, state* and indicates a _____.

acumen	enervate	isolation	obsession	repercussion
detriment	gratify	maintain	persona	riddle

WORK ADDICTION

Work addiction is a serious problem for two reasons: lack of understanding about the addiction and the **repercussions** of the addiction on both the addicts and those around them.

First, in order to understand work addiction, we need to understand the concept of healthy work and how it differs from work addiction. Healthy work provides a sense of identity, helps develop our strengths, and is a **gratifying** means of satisfaction, accomplishment, mastery of problems, and professional **acumen**. Healthy workers may work for long hours. Although they have occasional projects that keep them away from friends, family, and personal interests for short periods, they generally **maintain** balance in their lives and are in full control of their schedules. Healthy work does not consume the worker. Conversely, work addiction is the compulsive use of work to fulfill the needs of intimacy, power, and success. It is characterized by **obsession**, rigidity, fear, anxiety, low self-esteem, **isolation**, and the need to be perfect. Work addiction is more than being unable to relax when not doing something thought of as "productive." It is the pursuit of the "work **persona**," an image that work addicts wish to project onto others.

In addition to understanding the basic traits of work addiction, we must also understand the perilous effects it has on individuals and those around them. One area that is deeply affected is family life. Work addiction is a major source of marital problems and family breakups. In fact, most work addicts come from homes that were alcoholic, rigid, violent, or otherwise unhealthy. In addition to causing **detriment** to the family, work addiction takes a toll on people's emotional and physical health. They may become emotionally crippled. They lose the ability to connect with other people. They are often **riddled** with guilt and fear; they fear failure, and they fear their shortcomings will be discovered. Work addicts may also suffer several physical defects. For example, because they are unable to relax and play, they often suffer from chronic fatigue syndrome because the excessive work schedule **enervates** them. Work addicts suffer as well from digestive problems, and they often report feeling pressure in the chest, difficulty breathing, dizziness, and lightheadedness.

–Adapted from Rebecca J. Donatelle, *Access to Health,* 7th Edition. San Francisco: Benjamin Cummings, 2002, p. 318. Reprinted by permission of Pearson Education, Inc., Glenview, IL.

VISUAL VOCABULARY

Reading is a good escape and provides

a means for us to take on the _____ of the main character in the story and be someone else for a while.

  a. isolation
  b. persona

Susan Pongratz

EXERCISE **1** Context Clues

Refer to the previous passage and use context clues from the sentences below to determine the definition of each of the following words in **bold** print. Do not consult a dictionary.

1. acumen (ăk′yə-mən) n.
The business **acumen** of Donald Trump has helped him earn millions of dollars because he could discern opportunities for good investments.

_____ **Acumen** means
  a. insight.   c. failure.
  b. disappointment.   d. closeness.

2. detriment (dĕt′rə-mənt) n.
The mental **detriment** caused by the hurricane was evident when small children reportedly continued to have nightmares many months later.

_____ **Detriment** means
  a. compassion.   c. comfort.
  b. harm.   d. benefit.

3. enervate (ĕn′ər-vāt) v.
The heavy humidity and the almost unbearably high temperatures with no ocean breeze **enervated** us so much that all we wanted to do was lie in the sun and listen to the waves roll onshore.

_____ **Enervate** means
  a. exhaust.   c. distinguish.
  b. excite.   d. care for.

4. gratify (grăt′ə-fī′) v.

Although volunteer work may **gratify** the needs in a community, it also can satisfy a need in the volunteer to do something of value.

_____ **Gratify** means

    a. surround.   c. please.

    b. displease.   d. overwhelm.

5. isolation (ī′sə-lā′shən) n.

A devoted scientist who prefers to work alone, Dr. Knight spends many months in **isolation** in the Arctic studying nature in the hope of proving that global warming is a serious threat.

_____ **Isolation** means

    a. clusters.   c. harm.

    b. separation.   d. health.

6. maintain (mān-tān′) v.

In order to **maintain** his high 4.0 GPA, Charles decided to take sailing for P.E. credit, even though he was on the sailing team.

_____ **Maintain** means

    a. keep.   c. ruin.

    b. lose.   d. prevent.

7. obsession (əb-sĕsh′ən) n.

A manic love is characterized by extreme highs and lows, jealousy, and an unnatural and possessive **obsession** about the other person.

_____ **Obsession** means

    a. good manners.   c. fixation.

    b. sensitivity.   d. boredom.

8. persona (pər-sō′nə) n.

Our history teacher presents the **persona** of a dull, stodgy instructor in the classroom, but he is actually a fun-loving marathon runner who spends his free time snow boarding and dancing the tango.

_____ **Persona** means

    a. praise; fame.   c. ideal; perfection.

    b. discussion; lecture. d. image; role.

9. repercussion (rē′pər-kŭsh′ən) n.

When our college switched to online registration, there were initially some negative **repercussions** in enrollment because many students did not know how to use the new system.

_____ **Repercussion** means
a. beginning.   c. consequence.
b. arrangement.   d. cause.

10. riddle (rĭd′l) v.
After the hailstorm, Paul was upset to discover his soft-top Jeep was **riddled** with holes the size of golf balls.

_____ **Riddle** means
a. system.   c. puncture.
b. organized event.   d. puzzle.

EXERCISE 2 Word Sorts
Synonyms
Match the word to the synonyms or definitions that follow each blank.

1. _____ backlash; chain reaction; consequence; effect

2. _____ role; personality; image; impression

3. _____ preoccupation with an idea that often accompanies anxiety

4. _____ pierce; puncture; damage; pepper

5. _____ weaken; debilitate; sap your strength; exhaust

Antonyms
Select the letter of the word with the opposite meaning.

_____ **6.** isolation
a. separation   b. loneliness   c. eagerness   d. association

_____ **7.** gratify
a. reason   b. argue   c. displease   d. satisfy

_____ **8.** maintain
a. abandon   b. care for   c. nourish   d. exist

_____ **9.** detriment
a. harm   b. excitement   c. boredom   d. benefit

_____ **5.** acumen
a. skill   b. ignorance   c. illness   d. care

EXERCISE ❸ Fill in the Blank

Use context clues to determine the word that best completes each sentence.

1. The _____ an individual presents to the public is sometimes different from the personality a best friend sees.

2. To avoid future hurricane damage, many builders are now required to _____ stricter building codes such as using REBAR (steel reinforcing bar) for additional support.

3. Although she did not have all of the symptoms, the patient was diagnosed with fibromyalgia, a condition that _____ the patient, causing feelings of weakness and fatigue shortly after getting out of bed; however, with proper diet and stress management strategies, she learned ways to diminish the pain and improve the quality of her sleep.

4. Early each morning, we listened as the ivory-billed woodpecker _____ the dead oak tree nearby.

5. The prank on the football field seemed funny at the time; however, the _____ of the college administrator's anger no longer made it seem humorous.

6. In Nicholas Sparks' *The Wedding*, which is the sequel to *The Notebook*, Noah Calhoun's _____ with creating a rose garden of concentric hearts for Allie is another tender symbol of his love.

7. With a loan of only $10,000 and some excellent financial _____, the young couple tripled their investment within a year—enough to pay off the loan and make a down payment on their first home.

8. "Choose a career that will _____ your heart," Tom's grandmother said, "because of the good you can do rather than simply one that provides a lot of money but offers no personal satisfaction."

9. Because we are social creatures, forced _____ is a condition most humans find difficult to endure.

10. Submarine commanders require the crew to train constantly to prepare for any disaster that would be a _____ to the men's safety.

EXERCISE 4 Application

Using context clues, insert the vocabulary word in the appropriate blank. A part-of-speech clue is given for each vocabulary word.

In a recent study, scientists discovered Americans suffer more stress-related health problems than their British counterparts. The British live longer, and they pay less for health insurance as well.

Although business **(1)** (n.) _____ may account for the success of many at the top of the corporate ladder, American employers often require the same **(2)** (n.) _____ with success from their workers. Yet, trying to complete projects and meet deadlines often takes a perilous toll on workers' health.

Diseases such as diabetes, heart disease, stroke, cancer, lung disease, and high blood pressure are more prevalent in the United States than in Great Britain. Many health professionals believe that success at the **(3)** (n.) _____ of the workers is unacceptable. Although achievement can be **(4)** (v.) _____, it can also be deadly.

Many health professionals now recognize the mind–body connection implied in this study and thus suggest that the **(5)** (n.) _____ of overwork can be exhibited in many stress-related conditions.

Some of the symptoms can be diminished by learning relaxation techniques and dropping the **(6)** (n.) _____ of the driven executive **(7)** (v.) _____ with guilt if work is left undone at the end of the day. The Millennials—the new breed of college graduates—may have already begun to recognize ways to overcome the "fear of failure" mindset. This new generation is willing to **(8)** (v.) _____ a balance of work and play. Instead of developing a syndrome with symptoms of exhaustion and insomnia that can **(9)** (v.) _____ a person, they are more likely to turn down a promotion or a career of **(10)** (n.) _____ in an office cubicle and opt for jobs that are interesting and fun. For them, work is not all-consuming. They follow the advice of George Bernard Shaw, "We don't stop playing because we grow old; we grow old because we stop playing."

Stop and Think

Using at least three words from the list, summarize the passage in 50 words or less in the space below.

_____

_____

_____

_____

Go to **www.etymonline.com** and study the histories of the following words. Then fill in the blanks to complete the summaries.

1. acumen

In _____, the word *acumen* evolved from the _____ word _____, which means "to sharpen" and was subsequently used to mean "_____" or "_____."

2. gratify

Around _____, the word was used to mean "_____." It originally evolved from the _____ word *gratificari,* which was a combination of _____, "pleasing," and _____, "to make or perform."

3. persona

In _____, the word was first used to mean "outward or social personality" and had evolved from the _____ *persona,* which means _____. In _____, poet _____ used the word to mean "literary character representing voice of the author."

5 Vocabulary and Emotional Health

Get Ready to Read About Emotional Health

College health textbooks address issues that affect the whole person, including emotional health. This selection, which is on the topic of *love,* is an excerpt from a stress management textbook. As you read, connect the information to your personal experiences or to those of friends. Before you read, however, consider what you already know about the following word parts. The meanings of some have been provided. Recall what you learned in Chapter 1 and fill in the blanks for the others.

1. The prefix *ana-* means *upward, throughout.*

2. The prefix *com-* means *with, together.*

3. The prefix *con-* means _____.

4. The prefix *de-* means *down, from, away.*

5. The suffix *-able* means *able to* and indicates an _____.

6. The suffix *-cal* means *like, resembling* and indicates an _____.

7. The suffix *-fy* means _____ and indicates a _____.

8. The suffix *-ish* means _____ and indicates an _____.

9. The suffix *-ly* means *in a certain manner* and usually indicates an

   _____.

analytical	boon	conversely	diminish	methodical
apparent	comparable	defy	giddy	sustain

LOVE

Violins and valentines, roses and romance—this is the stuff relationships are made of. Or is it? Love itself completely **defies** definition. It is not a product of the logical, **methodical**, **analytical** left side of the brain. **Conversely,** love stems from the right side of the brain, which feels rather than thinks. Although the two sides of the brain do communicate well with each other, feelings cannot be described; only the expression or outwardly **apparent** behavior caused by the feeling can be explained. One of humanity's greatest frustrations throughout history has been the inability to define and explain feelings, especially love. That, of course, has been a **boon** to poets, Valentine's Day card manufacturers, florists, and others who make a living from our inability to convey the feelings we have for that special person in our life.

Love is like a stimulant drug. It lifts our spirits and makes us **giddy**, and the crash from a lost love is **comparable** to the depression that follows the withdrawal from a powerful drug. In between are the highs and lows that make our emotions feel like a rollercoaster ride. Actually, there are degrees and stages of love. Being in love occurs at the beginning of a relationship. After a period of time, the "in love" stage **diminishes**, and a couple either breaks up or develops what is referred to as second-stage or mature love. This is the kind of love that **sustains** a relationship or a marriage. Although everyone is capable of this type of love, some people never do accomplish or experience it.

–Adapted from Daniel A. Girdano, George S. Everly, Jr., and Dorothy E. Dusek, *Controlling Stress and Tension*, 6e, pp. 159-160. Published by Allyn and Bacon, Boston, MA. Copyright © 2001 by Pearson Education. Reprinted by permission of the publisher.

VISUAL VOCABULARY

This wedding couple is _____ with excitement on their wedding day.

  a. analytical
  b. giddy

George Pongratz

EXERCISE 1 Context Clues

Refer to the previous passage and use context clues from the sentences below to determine the definition of each of the following words in **bold** print. Do not consult a dictionary.

1. analytical (ăn′ə-lĭt′ĭk-ĭ-kəl) adj.
Einstein had such an **analytical** mind that when he was asked the location of his laboratory, he pointed to his head.

_____ **Analytical** means
- a. disorganized.
- b. logical.
- c. confused.
- d. simple.

2. apparent (ə-păr′ənt) adj.
As they observed the results of his hard training and amazing talent, it became quickly **apparent** to the fans that the newcomer to the Olympic games would be going home with a medal.

_____ **Apparent** means
- a. doubtful.
- b. hidden.
- c. unusual.
- d. obvious.

3. boon (bo͞on) n.
Just when there seemed to be a **boon** to the economy and gas prices began to fall, there was word that some Nigerian oil wells had been destroyed, which would then cause a negative effect on the world's financial situation.

_____ **Boon** means
- a. blessing.
- b. hardship.
- c. difficulty.
- d. curse.

4. comparable (kŏm′pər-ə-bəl) adj.
Although the two basketball teams are **comparable** in ability, one has more mental skill while the other seems to defeat itself psychologically.

_____ **Comparable** means
- a. careful.
- b. steady.
- c. equivalent.
- d. different.

5. conversely (kən-vûrs′-lē) adv.
Amy enjoys socializing so much that at the end of one party at midnight, she often searches for another; **conversely**, her shy sister is ready to leave any social event after twenty minutes.

_____ **Conversely** means
- a. in the opposite manner.
- b. in a similar manner.
- c. in a difficult manner.
- d. in a friendly manner.

6. defy (dĭ-fī′) v.

"My cats are not allowed to sleep on the furniture; however, they **defy** the family rules and end up on the sofa when everyone is out of sight," complained Vatanak.

_____ **Defy** means

a. frighten.
b. arrange.
c. simplify.
d. challenge.

7. diminish (dĭ-mĭn′ĭsh) v.

The enthusiasm of the fans quickly **diminished** when the point spread between the two teams grew larger and there no longer seemed to be a contest in the game.

_____ **Diminish** means

a. increase.
b. extend.
c. decrease.
d. make longer.

8. giddy (gĭd′ē) adj.

Having enjoyed too much pink champagne, the bridesmaids became **giddy**, and their giggling began to annoy some of the remaining guests.

_____ **Giddy** means

a. silly.
b. interested.
c. serious.
d. irritated.

9. methodical (mə-thŏd′ĭ-kəl) adj.

Francesca is so **methodical** that her career counselor suggested that she should consider a career in accounting, which requires a person to follow procedures and keep orderly records.

_____ **Methodical** means

a. angry.
b. lacking confidence.
c. in a disorderly manner.
d. in an orderly manner.

10. sustain (sə-stān′) v.

Karl practiced for months to qualify for the Boston Marathon, and once he knew he would be going, he worked to **sustain** that high level of conditioning he would need in the spring competition.

_____ **Sustain** means

a. smooth.
b. continue; maintain.
c. end.
d. rearrange.

EXERCISE **2** Word Sorts

Synonyms

Match the word to the synonyms or definitions that follow each blank.

1. _____ equivalent; tantamount; equal; proportionate

2. _____ blessing; advantage; good fortune; windfall

3. _____ examining; investigative; inquisitive; inquiring

4. _____ counter; against; contrarily; in reverse

5. _____ maintain; support; uphold; continue

Antonyms

Select the letter of the word with the opposite meaning.

_____ **6.** giddy

    a. serious   b. silly   c. artistic   d. organized

_____ **7.** methodical

    a. systematic   b. disorganized   c. political   d. legal

_____ **8.** apparent

    a. vague   b. obvious   c. realistic   d. dreamlike

_____ **9.** defy

    a. challenge   b. reorganize   c. obey   d. protest

_____ **10.** diminish

    a. reduce   b. expand   c. arrange   d. organize

EXERCISE **3** Fill in the Blank

Use context clues to determine the word that best completes each sentence.

1. Currently, coal is experiencing another _____ as scientists explore fuel sources that are alternatives to foreign oil.

2. To _____ her dog's attention during each training session, Kathryn has a pocketful of treats for rewards.

3. During his freshman year, Art failed to use his time wisely and ended up on academic probation; _____, after repeating two classes in the summer session, he has become focused and his grades reflect his new self-discipline.

4. It soon became _____ that marriage was in their future when Mike and Annie started spending more and more time together.

5. After listening to my description of my computer's problem, Simon, a student with an amazingly _____ mind, was able to figure out the solution.

6. Our enthusiasm for the movie slowly _____ when we realized we were surrounded by cell phone users.

7. His first trip backpacking was so good that he planned a second, with the hopes that it would be a _____ experience.

8. Because of her talent for _____ organization, Sandra considered a career in project management.

9. In spite of his premature birth, Joey _____ the predictions of the doctors and, after years of rehabilitation and physical therapy, he leads a normal, independent life.

10. Although people with acrophobia are fearful of heights, others feel happy and even somewhat _____ at high levels.

EXERCISE 4 Application

Using context clues, insert the vocabulary word in the appropriate blank. A part-of-speech clue is given for each.

Acupuncture is one of the oldest medical procedures still being used. Originating in China more than 2,000 years ago, it grew in acceptance in the United States in 1971 after *New York Times* reporter James Reston wrote about how doctors in China used needles to **(1)** (v.) _____ his post-surgery pain. As a result, the medical community began investigating acupuncture in an **(2)** (adj.) _____ way to determine its applications. Following Reston's report, it became **(3)** (adj.) _____ that acupuncture could **(4)** (v.) defy some previously held notions about alternative medicine and **(5)** (adj.) _____ techniques in that field.

Currently, the acupuncture technique that has been studied in organized, **(6)** (adj.) _____ ways in the United States involves penetrating the skin with thin, solid, metallic needles that are manipulated by the hands or by electrical stimulation.

In the past two decades, acupuncture has experienced a **(7)** (n.) _____ in popularity in the United States and is widely practiced by physicians, dentists, acupuncturists, and other practitioners for relief or prevention of pain and other diseases, including fibromyalgia, osteoarthritis, addiction, stroke rehabilitation, headache, tennis elbow, low-back pain, carpal tunnel syndrome, and asthma.

The sensation people feel from the needles varies from no feeling to minimal pain. Some people are energized by the treatment so that they almost feel **(8)** (adj.) _____ and extremely happy, while others become very relaxed. **(9)** (adv.) _____, with improper needle placement, a patient's movement during the procedure, or a defect in the needle, a person can **(10)** (v.) _____ soreness and pain. Therefore, it is imperative to seek treatment from a qualified acupuncturist.

—Adapted from "Acupuncture," *Get the Facts*,
National Center for Complementary and Alternative
Medicine (Retrieved 7–14–06) National Institutes of
Health nccam.nih.gov

Stop and Think

Using at least three words from the list, summarize the passage about love in 50 words or less in the space below.

_____

_____

_____

_____

_____

Study the images and then write the word that best connects to each picture. Then write a sentence explaining your rationale.

Courtesy of Microsoft.

1._____

_____

_____

Courtesy of Microsoft.

2._____

_____

_____

_____

Courtesy of Microsoft.

3._____

_____

_____

Courtesy of Microsoft.

4._____

_____

_____

Courtesy of Microsoft.

5._____

_____

_____

6

Vocabulary and Medical Ethics

Get Ready to Read About Medical Ethics

In addition to lab sciences and nursing courses, students in the nursing program are required to take a course in ethics, which involves the study of moral choices. As you can imagine, the field of medicine involves daily critical decisions—many of which require nurses to determine what is right or wrong for the patient, the family, and the community. Before you read the following selection from a nursing textbook, consider what you already know about the following word parts. The meanings of some have been provided. Recall what you learned in Chapter 1 and fill in the blanks for the others.

1. The prefix *auto-* means _____.

2. The prefix *com-* means _____.

3. The prefix *con-* means _____.

4. The prefix *di-* means _____.

5. The root *cede* means *go, lead, yield.*

6. The root *lemma* means *proposition.*

7. The suffix *-tion* means _____ and indicates a _____.

| autonomy | constraint | ethical | integrity | precedent |
| collaboration | dilemma | hinder | intuition | principle |

MAKING ETHICAL DECISIONS

Responsible **ethical** reasoning is rational and systematic. It should be based on ethical **principles** and codes rather than on emotions, **intuition**, fixed policies, or **precedent** (that is, an earlier similar occurrence).

A good decision is one that is in the client's best interest and at the same time preserves the **integrity** of all involved. Nurses have ethical obligations to their clients, to the agency that employs them and to physicians. Therefore, nurses must weigh competing factors when making ethical decisions. Although ethical reasoning is principle based and has the client's well-being at center, being involved in ethical problems and **dilemmas** is stressful for the nurse. The nurse may feel torn between obligations to the client, the family, and the employer. What is in the client's best interest may be contrary to the nurse's personal belief system. In settings in which ethical decisions arise frequently, nurses should establish support systems such as team conferences and use of counseling professionals to allow expression of their feelings.

Although the nurse's input is important, in reality several people are usually involved in making an ethical decision. Therefore, **collaboration,** communication, and compromise are important skills for health professionals. When nurses do not have the **autonomy** to act on their moral or ethical choices, compromise becomes essential.

Several strategies help nurses overcome possible organizational and social **constraints** that may **hinder** the ethical practice of nursing and create moral distress for nurses.

—From Barbara Kozier, Glenora Erb, Audrey Berman, and Shirlee Snyder, *Fundamentals of Nursing,* 7th Edition, pp. 76-77. © 2004. Reprinted by permission of Pearson Education, Inc., Upper Saddle River, NJ.

VISUAL VOCABULARY

These college students are working in

_____, cooperatively sharing their ideas to complete a project.

a. autonomy
b. collaboration

Courtesy of Microsoft.

EXERCISE 1 Context Clues

Refer to the previous passage and use context clues from the sentences below to determine the definition of each of the following words in **bold** print. Do not consult a dictionary.

1. autonomy (ô-tŏn′ə-mē) n.
   Citizens of the small region that had been oppressed by the current government sought **autonomy** because they believed their independence and freedom would provide relief and happiness.

   _____ **Autonomy** means
   - a. money.
   - b. power.
   - c. independence.
   - d. dependence.

2. collaboration (kə-lăb′ə-rā′-shən) n.
   "A **collaboration** of the marketing and design departments," announced the corporation president, "has helped us win the Primo Prize, the highest award in our field—proof that great ideas are a combination of many good ideas."

   _____ **Collaboration** means
   - a. act of writing details.
   - b. act of working jointly.
   - c. competition.
   - d. act of working in isolation.

3. constraint (kən-strānt′) n.
   In spite of the **constraint** of having no family support and very little money, Alex will graduate in May and enter law school in the fall.

   _____ **Constraint** means
   - a. restriction.
   - b. freedom.
   - c. scholarship.
   - d. advice.

4. dilemma (dĭ-lĕm′ə) n.
   Steven faced a **dilemma:** stay in his current job, which offered a chance of a promotion within five years or go to graduate school and improve his chances of getting an even better job in two years.

   _____ **Dilemma** means
   - a. opportunity.
   - b. promotion.
   - c. difficult choice.
   - d. obstacle.

5. ethical (ĕth′ĭ-kəl) adj.
Unless a person has a DNR—do not resuscitate—order, paramedics called on the scene cannot make the **ethical** decision about whether they should allow the patient to die; consequently, they will go to great measures to save the patient.

_____ **Ethical** means
   a. relating to ideas of right and wrong.
   b. aware.
   c. simple.
   d. relating to an obvious choice.

6. hinder (hīn′dər) v.
Michael realized that a weak background in math would **hinder** his progress in chemistry, so he decided to take a refresher course in precalculus first.

_____ **Hinder** means
   a. maintain.   c. improve.
   b. encourage.   d. prevent.

7. integrity (ĭn-tĕg′rĭ-tē) n.
Although the decision to tell the truth was difficult and would have serious repercussions, Raymond showed **integrity** by admitting his mistake and taking responsibility for his actions.

_____ **Integrity** means
   a. dishonesty.   c. fear.
   b. honesty.   d. reaction.

8. intuition (ĭn′too-ĭsh′ən) n.
Jean had no scientific reason to be afraid in the new house; instead, her fear was based on **intuition**, and a similar feeling in the past had proved accurate.

_____ **Intuition** means
   a. observation based on obvious facts.
   b. sense of something.
   c. idea based on instruction.
   d. fear.

9. precedent (prĕs′ĭ-dənt) n.
Because of a **precedent** made in an earlier court decision, the judge ruled in favor of the plaintiff.

_____ **Precedent** means
a. new decision.
b. example from an earlier decision.
c. argument.
d. decision without basis.

10. principle (prĭn′sə-pəl) n.
One **principle** that Americans believe in is the importance of treating others fairly.

_____ **Principle** means
a. government.
b. manner.
c. art.
d. basic truth.

EXERCISE **2** Word Sorts

Synonyms

Match the word to the synonyms or definitions that follow each blank.

1. _____ cooperation; association; affiliation; concord

2. _____ prevent; thwart; restrict; impede

3. _____ example; model; paradigm; criterion

4. _____ law; assumption; belief; ideal

5. _____ prescience; ESP; feeling; premonition

Antonyms

Select the letter of the word(s) with the opposite meaning.

_____ **6.** integrity
a. dishonesty　b. honesty　c. uprightness　d. expectation

_____ **7.** ethical
a. moral　b. immoral　c. managing　d. misdirected

_____ **8.** dilemma
a. snap decision　b. difficult choice　c. conundrum　d. trick

_____ **9.** autonomy
a. self-reliance　b. independence　c. authority　d. dependence

_____ **10.** constraint
a. restriction　b. barrier　c. obstacle　d. freedom

EXERCISE **3** Fill in the Blank

Use context clues to determine the word that best completes each sentence.

1. The new company president lives by the _____ of hard work, fairness, and valuing her employees.

2. The _____ of students in the newly formed learning community has created a sense of belonging and cooperation that also encourages academic success.

3. Kim faced a _____: Should she risk her friendship and report her roommate for cheating, or should she overbook the truth and pretend no cheating occurred.

4. After they bought their son a used car when he got his first job, my neighbors realized they had set a _____ that would eventually require them to do the same for their other two children.

5. The obstacle that _____ their relationship was that Tom wanted to get married as soon as they graduated, but his girlfriend wanted to pursue her career first and experience living on her own in another city.

6. In our philosophy class, we often discuss _____ questions that may not have a definite right or wrong answer, but we are always required to back up our claim with specific support from our readings.

7. My _____ is as good as a global positioning system because I always seem to get the right feeling about which way to go.

8. The financial _____ of taking on a mortgage can be restrictive at first, but the future rewards of the investment make the sacrifice worth it.

9. Children begin to seek _____ when they are two years old—independently exploring, investigating, and sometimes defying their parents' rules.

10. The building inspector showed his _____ after he examined the structure and refused to approve its faulty wiring and substandard workmanship.

EXERCISE 4 Application

Using context clues, insert the vocabulary word in the appropriate blank. A part-of-speech clue is given for each vocabulary word.

Medical research makes great progress each year in discovering more about diseases and their potential cures. Still, **(1)** (adj.) _____ issues arise as we anticipate problems, which often present new **(2)** (n.) _____. One example is cloning.

In a **(3)** (n.) _____, Ian Wilmut and his associates at the Roslin Institute in Edinburgh, Scotland, set a new medical **(4)** (n.) _____ in cloning research. Through their precise calculations, scientific theory, and personal **(5)** (n.) _____, the scientists proved that "cell specialization is possible under the right conditions."

No longer **(6)** (v.) _____ by the mistakes restricting previous researchers and determined to successfully perform the experiment with **(7)** (n.) _____ and honesty, the team cloned the now famous sheep Dolly from the cells of a six-year-old ewe (female sheep).

The moral issue? Dolly soon developed health problems usually attributed to older sheep. Recent studies have since indicated that Dolly may have been born middle-aged. Critics believe researchers should work under the **(8)** (n.) _____ and boundary of the idea that all creatures deserve an equal chance at a good quality of life. They believe cloning recklessly and selfishly uses the lives of animals, and that the potential for abnormalities resulting from the process are great. Thus, to them cloning is immoral.

Supporters of the procedure, on the other hand, believe that genetic engineering can be used for good. The cloning process, they contend, may provide ways to increase the population of endangered species. It may also increase food supplies in Third World countries, thus adding to their **(9)** (n.) _____ and reducing their dependence on more powerful nations. They recognize the

(10) (n.) _____ of the medical community, "Do no harm." But they also believe the procedure could lead to great progress.

While the debate continues, so does the research.

Stop and Think

 Write words derived from the given word part that match the definitions provided. You may need to consult a dictionary.

Auto- (Greek) "Self"	*Integer* (Latin) "Whole"
1._____ : a self-propelled vehicle	1._____ : unite
2._____ : robot-like person	2._____ : whole number
3._____ : involuntary	3._____ : essential to completeness
4._____ : independent	4._____ : break into parts

Study the images and then write the word that best connects to each picture. Then write a sentence explaining your rationale.

Courtesy of Microsoft.

1._____

Courtesy of Microsoft.

2._____

Courtesy of Microsoft.

3._____

Courtesy of Microsoft.

4._____

Vocabulary and Nursing

Get Ready to Read About Nursing

Textbooks on nursing and health care focus on topics about the concepts, processes, and practices of nursing. Ranging from Clara Barton to current events topics about global health, the subjects cover a wide range. Students in nursing programs need a strong background knowledge in the sciences. They also require prior knowledge of word parts because many medical terms are derived from Latin and Greek words.

Before you read the following selection on the concept of homeostasis, consider what you already know about the following word parts. The meanings of some have been provided. Recall what you learned in Chapter 1 and fill in the blanks for the others.

1. The prefix *en-* means *to make.*

2. The prefix *inter-* means _____.

3. The prefix *per-* means _____.

4. The root *holos* means *whole.*

5. The root *homos* means *same.*

6. The root *venire* means *to come.*

7. The suffix *-ism* means *theory, system, doctrine* and usually indicates a noun.

| assess | dynamics | entity | homeostasis | perception |
| dimension | encompass | holism | intervene | regimen |

HOMEOSTASIS

Nurses **assess** and plan health care for three types of clients: the individual, the family, and the community. Care of the individual is enhanced when the nurse understands the concepts of individuality, **holism, homeostasis,** human needs, and systems theory. The beliefs and values of each person and the support he or she receives come in large part from the family and are reinforced by the community. Thus an understanding of family **dynamics** and the context of the community assist the nurse in planning care. When the family is the client, the nurse determines the health status of the family and its individual members, the level of family functioning, family interaction patterns, and family strengths and weaknesses. When a community is the client, the nurse determines what environmental problems are present—for example, pollution, poor sanitation, waste disposal, incidence of crime, housing conditions, and so on—and **intervenes** to promote a **regimen** of healthful living and to prevent health problems.

Dimensions of individuality include the person's total character, self-identity, and **perceptions.** The person's total character **encompasses** behaviors, emotional state, attitudes, values, motives, abilities, habits, and appearances. The person's self-identity encompasses perception of self as a separate and distinct **entity** alone and in interactions with others. The person's perceptions encompass the way the person interprets the environment or situation, directly affecting how the person thinks, feels, and acts in any given situation.

—Adapted from Barbara Kozier, Glenora Erb, Audrey Berman, and Shirlee Snyder, *Fundamentals of Nursing,* 7th Edition, p. 188. © 2004. Reprinted by permission of Pearson Education, Inc., Upper Saddle River, NJ.

VISUAL VOCABULARY

Before prescribing any medication, this doctor

will _____ the patient's health.

a. assess
b. intervene

Courtesy of Microsoft.

EXERCISE 1 Context Clues

Refer to the previous passage and use context clues from the sentences below to determine the definition of each of the following words in **bold** print. Do not consult a dictionary.

1. assess (ə-sĕs′) v.

Before doctors can prescribe medication, they **assess** a patient's health to determine the proper treatment based on medical tests.

_____ **Assess** means

a. arrange.   c. cure.

b. evaluate.   d. relieve.

2. dimension (dĭ-mĕn′shən) n.

One **dimension** of a healthy lifestyle is a proper diet.

_____ **Dimension** means

a. percentage.   c. food.

b. randomness.   d. aspect.

3. dynamics (dī-năm′ĭks) n.

The **dynamics** of our history class are so positively charged that we are able to have lively, but friendly debates.

_____ **Dynamics** means

a. force and energy.   c. circles.

b. imitation.   d. records and reasons.

4. encompass (ĕn-kŭm′pəs) v.

Our learning community **encompasses** courses in psychology, art, and interpersonal communication.

_____ **Encompass** means

a. reject.   c. include.

b. relieve.   d. exclude.

5. entity (ĕn′tĭ-tē) n.

The speaker scanned the crowded auditorium and studied individuals, recognizing each person as a unique **entity**, rather than just a part of the huge mass.

_____ **Entity** means

a. individual being.   c. guest.

b. crowd.   d. endangered species.

6. holism (hō′lĭz′əm) n.
Scientific study has presented the idea of **holism,** which makes us recognize how things are interconnected.

_____ **Holism** means
   a. belief that living matter consists of wholes that are greater than the sum of their parts.
   b. something sacred.
   c. satisfaction in an accomplishment.
   d. belief that life consists of serious consequences, usually without joy.

7. homeostasis (hō′mē-ō-stā′sĭs) n.
Following surgery, the doctors waited to determine if **homeostasis** had been achieved and the patient was stabilized before they made a prognosis.

_____ **Homeostasis** means
   a. illness.   c. excessive bleeding.
   b. internal balance.   d. increased pain.

8. intervene (ĭn′tər-vēn′) v.
To avoid a major argument, the referees **intervened** and called technical fouls on both teams.

_____ **Intervene** means
   a. reach.   c. prevent.
   b. come between.   d. punish.

9. perception (pər-sĕp′shən) n.
Because we live in a visual age and we are surrounded by images, much of what we believe is based on **perception** and how others see things rather than reality.

_____ **Perception** means
   a. view or image.   c. detail.
   b. reality.   d. accurate information.

10. regimen (rĕj′ə-mən) n.
By following a **regimen** of daily walking and healthful eating, Emily lost ten pounds over the summer.

_____ **Regimen** means
   a. irregular attempt.   c. strict practice.
   b. unrealistic dream.   d. sneaky preview.

EXERCISE 2 Word Sorts

Synonyms

Match the word to the synonyms or definitions that follow each blank.

1. _____ belief that the whole equals more than the sum of the parts

2. _____ energy; action; progress; exchange

3. _____ view; understanding; attitude; concept

4. _____ aspect; feature; range; scope

5. _____ routine; plan; program; procedure

Antonyms

Select the letter of the word(s) with the opposite meaning.

_____ 6. intervene
   a. accept   b. avoid   c. come between d. comfort

_____ 7. encompass
   a. surround   b. envelope   c. leave   d. arrange

_____ 8. homeostasis
   a. imbalance b. balance   c. authority   d. prediction

_____ 9. assess
   a. evaluate   b. neglect   c. attack   d. access

_____ 10. entity
   a. character   b. individual c. crowd   d. religion

EXERCISE 3 Fill in the Blank

Use context clues to determine the word that best completes each sentence.

1. When contract negotiations hit a dead end, a third party _____ to help the two sides reach a compromise.

2. A course in humanities may _____ readings in art, literature, music, and religion.

3. A key comprehension strategy is to _____ your background knowledge of a subject as you preview a passage.

4. By following a strict vegan _____ of fruits and vegetables and eliminating all meat, fish, poultry, and animal products such as eggs, milk or cheese, my cousin is trying to lower his LDL cholesterol.

5. The goal of any EMT is to stabilize the patient during transport and then hope the hospital staff can establish long-term _____.

6. Because the students had established such a sense of community with energizing _____, the professor was able to use group work successfully in each lecture.

7. In Stephen King's *The Girl Who Loved Tom Gordon,* the reader is aware of an unknown evil _____ watching as the young girl continues to wander deeper into the woods.

8. The vision statement of the corporation is an example of _____ because it focuses on the whole person, thus encouraging lifelong learning, physical health, and building of strong emotional ties.

9. When he received his first compass as a young boy, Albert Einstein realized the magnetic field proved there were other _____ in the universe besides the ones we could see.

10. Knowing that the debates were an important aspect of winning the election, Glenn studied the issues carefully and prepared his responses to ensure that the voters would have the _____ that he was the best candidate.

EXERCISE 4 Application

Using context clues, insert the vocabulary word in the appropriate blank. A part-of-speech clue is given for each vocabulary word.

A major concern of community health is how to avoid or deal with a pandemic (that is, widespread disease affecting a large population). The possibility of an outbreak of influenza such as the 1918 Spanish flu that **(1)** (v.) _____ a large population has recently generated discussions among health professionals worldwide. They are working on a program to **(2)** (v.) _____ and treat patients quickly as well as determining ways to prevent panic. The **(3)** (n.) _____ of the discussions also center around how all health professionals can collaborate to diminish the effects of a major outbreak. During the discussions, the disease becomes an evil **(4)** (n.) _____, the enemy that must be outwitted and overcome—much like the relentless robot T-1000 in *Terminator II.*

Avian flu, also known as *bird flu, avian influenza,* and *bird influenza,* is currently one of those entities. Although it is caused by a virus adapted to birds, it has been known to cross species and has affected humans in several countries.

As the issue becomes widely publicized and public awareness increases, the **(5)** (n.) _____ of danger must be reduced to avoid panic. To prevent widespread alarm, the media is educating communities about ways to **(6)** (v.) _____ in the case of an outbreak. For one, consider the **(7)** (n.) _____ required for optimum health: balanced diet, exercise, good personal hygiene, and proper hand washing. The concept of **(8)** (n.) _____, then, is important not only to the whole person but also to the whole community.

Doctors are also stressing that current medical resources make dealing with a flu outbreak less dangerous than in 1918 because of antibiotics and practices to avoid dehydration. Thus, **(9)** (n.) _____ of an individual's vital signs can be obtained more rapidly than in the previous century. Every **(10)** (n.) _____ and factor of avoiding and controlling outbreaks of the disease is being considered because in our global society, the health of one person affects the health of everyone.

Stop and Think

 Go to **http://virus.stanford.edu/uda/** and read about the 1918 Spanish flu, then on your own paper write your impressions of the pandemic.

 Go to **www.etymonline** to answer the following.

1. What is the definition of the Greek word *pan* in pandemic?

_____

2. What is the definition of the Greek word *demos* in pandemic?

_____

3. What is the definition of the Greek word *epi* in epidemic?

_____

4. What do you suppose is the difference in a pandemic and an epidemic?

_____

UNIT 2

Review Test
Chapters 3–7

1 Word Parts

Match the definitions in Column 2 to the word parts in Column 1.

Column 1

_____ **1.** grat

_____ **2.** auto

_____ **3.** -able

_____ **4.** di-

_____ **5.** -ous

_____ **6.** pre-

_____ **7.** -ate

_____ **8.** -tion

_____ **9.** com-

_____ **10.** -ish

Column 2

a. self

b. like

c. action; state

d. before

e. pleasing

f. with; together

g. capable of

h. cause to become

i. related to; full of

j. two

2 Fill in the Blank

Use context clues to determine the best word from the box to complete each sentence.

apparent	detriment	entity	prevalence	riddle
conversely	dimension	obsession	principle	sustain

1. Even as a young man, Albert Einstein was beginning to think beyond the _____ of this world when he imagined what it would be like to ride a beam of light.

2. After deciding to go to Jalalabad to help the local farmers, Keith was suddenly _____ with doubt when he realized he was like the man in the Paul Simon song who was a stranger who did not speak the language and did not know the currency.

3. How can we encourage college students to avoid experiences that are a _____ to their health and that endanger their lives, such as binge drinking and cigarette smoking?

4. Trying to _____ a relationship over a long distance, Adam had a large cell phone bill; unfortunately, now he did not have enough money to fly out and see Jane.

5. Because of the _____ of cheating in academic settings, professors now use online resources to track down original sources.

6. Although each was a distinct _____, people frequently confused the twins, so they began to dress differently and participate in separate activities on campus.

7. Playing the online war craft game became such an _____ for Cecil that he ended up on academic probation because he had spent his time on the Internet when he should have been studying.

8. It was _____ to us that Megan was involved with a very manipulative boyfriend when he always came to her for help whenever he had a writing assignment.

9. Jake worked on the school newspaper and was an active member of the Young Republicans; _____, his brother Josh competed on the wrestling team and was a member of the Young Democrats.

10. According to motivational speaker Robert Collier, "The first _____ of success is desire."

3 Book Connection

Use context clues to determine the best word from the box to complete each sentence.

analytical	diminish	hinder	homeostasis	maintain
despite	ethical	holism	intuition	obtain

THE BIG PICTURE

At the beginning of his book, Dr. Benjamin Carson describes a surgery he was asked to perform to separate craniopagus twins—boys conjoined at the head. Following the surgery, the team of doctors and nurses keep close vigil on the babies' vital signs, hoping for **(1)** (n.) _____. Unfortunately, because the twins are symbiotic—that is, they share some of the same organs for survival—the medical team is not able to **(2)** (v.) _____ stability, and the babies die.

Although this may seem like a negative opening, Carson presents his talent, his anecdotes about overcoming personal obstacles, and his observations about living life with honesty, kindness, and integrity. He is an **(3)** (adj.) _____ human being who understands personal struggle, but he is also one who believes you should not steal someone's struggle. Growth and success can eventually emerge from failure.

Throughout his own disappointments, Dr. Carson retains a close relationship with God. A vegetarian, family man, devoted husband, son, and father, he strives to exhibit **(4)** (n.) _____ in all aspects of his life. For him, that wholeness leads to living a genuine life.

Interwoven in the medical language of this nonfiction book is Carson's own personal story. He and his brother Curtis were headed for trouble until their mother prayed for guidance in handling the dilemma: Should she allow them the freedom to continue, or should she take drastic measures to take control? **(5)** (prep.) _____ her sons' protests, Sonya Carson intervened in their lives and set new boundaries. By limiting their television viewing and requiring them to read and report on two library books each week, she based her plan on her personal **(6)** (n.) _____ and feelings as well as a plan from a Higher Power.

The plan worked. Through reading and more focused studying, the boys became excellent students. Although distractions had previously **(7)** (v.) _____ their success, eventually there was less to prevent them from earning good grades. They developed better vocabularies, increased their background knowledge on a variety of subjects, and became more **(8)** (adj.) _____ about ways to approach obstacles.

The book is not just the story of how Carson became the chief of pediatric neurosurgery at Johns Hopkins Hospital in Baltimore, Maryland. It is also a platform for his ideas about fighting the "victim mentality"—learning to solve problems rather than blaming someone else. It is also about the importance of having good manners and being nice. In addition, Carson discusses other people who have overcome difficulty to **(9)** (v.) _____ success.

Finally, the book is about world issues as well. At a time when many people have begun to feel **(10)** (v.) _____ by barriers such as poverty or the lack of opportunities, Dr. Carson provides a new perspective, explaining that they should not allow the difficulties to make them feel less. Conversely, they should see each hindrance as an opportunity—a chance to grow.

4 Visual Connection

Write a caption for this picture using two of the words from the box.

comparable	constraint	deviant	enervate	isolation
compulsiveness	denigrate	deprive	grave	repercussion

Courtesy of Microsoft.

_____

_____

_____

_____

_____

_____

_____

_____

5 Analogies

Choose the word that best completes the analogy.

1. water : energy :: personalities : _____
   a. dynamics   b. integrity   c. acumen

2. question : interview :: evaluate : _____
   a. collaborate   b. assess   c. defy

3. opponents : debate :: partners : _____
   a. defy   b. assess   c. collaboration

4. rule : break :: law : _____
   a. defy   b. assess   c. collaborate

5. failure : foolishness :: success : _____
   a. acumen   b. entity   c. isolation

2

6. sad : gloomy :: silly : _____
    a. methodical   b. giddy   c. grave

7. cause : effect :: action : _____
    a. acumen   b. integrity   c. ramification

8. stock market crash : depression :: gold rush : _____
    a. integrity   b. dynamics   c. boon

9. dishonesty : immorality :: honesty : _____
    a. acumen   b. ramification   c. integrity

10. artist : creative :: accountant : _____
    a. giddy   b. methodical   c. grave

CHAPTER

8

Vocabulary and Sociology

Get Ready to Read About Sociology

Sociology is the study of human behavior within societies. During a course in sociology, you will study about other cultures and how people within those cultures interact. You will also study about the values, customs, and traditions held by people worldwide. Before you read the selection, consider the word parts you already know and fill in the blanks. The meanings of some have been provided. Recall what you learned in Chapter 1 and fill in the blanks for the others.

1. The prefix *di-* means _____.

2. The prefix *pre-* means _____.

3. The prefix *sub-* means _____.

4. The suffix *-ity* means *quality, trait* and indicates a _____.

| acknowledge | civilian | intensity | protocol | subculture |
| bestow | diversion | precise | sneer | thrust |

BOOT CAMP AS A TOTAL INSTITUTION

The bus arrives at Parris Island, South Carolina, at 3 A.M. The early hour is no accident. The recruits are groggy, confused. Up to a few hours ago, the boys were ordinary **civilians**. Now, a sergeant **sneers** and calls them "maggots," their heads are buzzed (25 seconds per recruit), and they are **thrust** quickly into the harsh world of Marine boot camp.

Buzzing the boys' hair is just the first step in stripping away their identity so the Marines can stamp a new one in its place. The uniform serves the same purpose. So does the ban on using the first person "I." Even a simple request must be made in **precise** Marine **protocol** or it will not be **acknowledged**. ("Sir, Recruit Jones requests permission to make a head call, Sir.")

Every intense moment of the next eleven weeks reminds the recruits that they are joining a **subculture** of self-discipline. Here pleasure is suspect and sacrifice is good. As they learn the Marine way of talking, walking, and thinking, they are denied **diversions** they once took for granted: television, cigarettes, cars, candy, soft drinks, video games, music, alcohol, drugs, and sex.

Lessons are **bestowed** with fierce **intensity**. When Sgt. Carey checks brass belt buckles, Recruit Robert Shelton nervously blurts, "I don't have one." Sgt. Carey's face grows red as the veins in his neck bulge. "I?" he says, his face just inches from his mouth, he screams, " 'I' is gone!"

"Nobody's an individual" is the lesson that is driven home again and again. "You are a team, a Marine. Not a civilian. Not black or white, but a Marine. You will live like a Marine, fight like a Marine, and, if necessary, die like a Marine."

—Adapted from James M. Henslin, *Essentials of Sociology,* 5e, p. 73. Published by Allyn and Bacon, Boston, MA. Copyright © 2004 by Pearson Education. Reprinted by permission of the publisher.

VISUAL VOCABULARY

Playing basketball is a good _____ for college students to enjoy in their spare time.

a. intensity
b. diversion

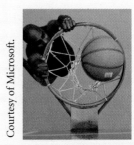

Courtesy of Microsoft.

EXERCISE **1** Context Clues

Refer to the previous passage and use context clues from the sentences below to determine the definition of each of the following words in **bold** print. Do not consult a dictionary.

1. acknowledge (ăk-nŏl′ĭj) v.
At the annual sports banquet, our coach **acknowledged** the families of the players who supported the team and contributed to their success.

_____ **Acknowledge** means
a. ignore.   c. recognize.
b. make calm.   d. refuse.

2. bestow (bĭ-stō′) v.
Grooms sometimes **bestow** the honor of best man on the father.

_____ **Bestow** means
a. take.   c. remove.
b. withhold.   d. give.

3. civilian (sĭ-vĭl′yən) n.
After graduation from college, Ian gave up his life as a **civilian** for a career in the army and headed to boot camp.

_____ **Civilian** means
a. private citizen.   c. officer.
b. military personnel.   d. administrator.

4. diversion (dĭ-vûr′zhən) n.
Successful people recognize the importance of hard work as well as the need to make time for **diversions** such as exercising, gardening, traveling, or reading for pleasure.

_____ **Diversion** means
a. pastime.   c. work experience.
b. boredom.   d. discussion.

5. intensity (ĭn-tĕn′sĭ-tē) n.
Tony felt the sudden loss of his wife with such **intensity** that for a year, he wore only black and showed no joy in life.

_____ **Intensity** means
a. unconcern.   c. joy.
b. coldness.   d. depth.

6. precise (prĭ-sīs′) adj.
Elizabeth's piano teacher demands that she practice daily so that her final juried performance will be **precise** and without mistakes.

_____ **Precise** means

a. exact.   c. silent.

b. inaccurate.   d. uncertain.

7. protocol (prō′tə-kôl′) n.
While Dave was at the U.S. Naval Academy, he was drilled in proper etiquette and military **protocol**, so he would be able to follow the accepted procedures at any formal function.

_____ **Protocol** means

a. subject.   c. disagreement.

b. procedure.   d. informality.

8. sneer (snîr) v.
When Janie held up the computer mouse and clicked it like a TV remote, the technology expert sitting nearby **sneered** at her and said, "Uh, duh, you need to keep it on the desk for it to work."

_____ **Sneer** means

a. mock.   c. express admiration.

b. admire.   d. to please.

9. subculture (sŭb′kŭl′chər) n.
The local high school had a growing population and within the student body were several **subcultures,** including the athletes, the science experts, the computer gurus, and the drama groupies.

_____ **Subculture** means

a. public organization.   c. total population.

b. science club.   d. small community.

10. thrust (thrəst) v.
Front seat airbags help prevent a person from being **thrust** into the windshield in the event of an impact.

_____ **Thrust** means

a. move gently.   c. surround.

b. push with force.   d. avoid.

EXERCISE **2** Word Sorts

Synonyms

Match the word to the synonyms or definitions that follow each blank.

1. _____ recreation; amusement; pastime

2. _____ move forward; advance; push

3. _____ cluster from a larger group who share common traits

4. _____ power; sharpness; emotion

5. _____ formality; ceremony; conformity

Antonyms

Select the letter of the word(s) with the opposite meaning.

_____ **6.** acknowledge
   a. recognize   c. discuss
   b. accept   d. deny

_____ **7.** precise
   a. inaccurate   c. clear
   b. exact   d. specific

_____ **8.** bestow
   a. give   c. devote
   b. deprive   d. present

_____ **9.** civilian
   a. noncombatant   c. soldier
   b. private citizen   d. private contractor

_____ **10.** sneer
   a. stare   c. express disgust
   b. praise   d. show disrespect

EXERCISE **3** Fill in the Blank

Use context clues to determine the word that best completes each sentence.

1. Living life as a _____ was very different for Barrett, who had spent 30 years as a CIA operative traveling to exotic destinations.

2. Trey said that working as an intern at the hospital was so time-consuming and exhausting that his only _____ was sleep.

3. The Joker _____ at Batman and expressed disgust for the superhero who had fallen for the trap.

4. After the sudden death of the college president, the entire campus was

_____ into a state of despair over the loss.

5. During the conference with his philosophy professor, Jerry

_____ that he was not keeping up with the assignments because of his part-time job.

6. A glassblower's timing must be _____ in order to prevent distorted shapes or shattered art.

7. Although he did not like going to the doctor, the pain from his migraine

increased to an _____ that finally prompted Hollis to make an appointment.

8. The _____ of fraternities and sororities can provide a sense of belonging to students on a large college campus.

9. After the funeral, Arline _____ her father's treasured gold pocket watch on the eldest grandson.

10. Before the governor arrived by helicopter, representatives of the

community were advised on the _____ for asking questions during the town meeting.

EXERCISE 4 Application

Using context clues, insert the vocabulary word in the appropriate blank. A part-of-speech clue is given for each vocabulary word.

The commissioning of the submarine *Hampton* began with a formal

gala at the National Air and Space Museum, hosted by the ship's captain,

Dave Antanitus. Also in attendance was the honorary chair, author Tom

Clancy, who **(1)** (v.) _____ that some of his previous visits to

the sub had been for research he was conducting for a new book. Clancy is

known for including **(2)** (adj.) _____ and very accurate details

in his techno-thrillers.

Because the event was a formal ball, strict military **(3)** (n.) _____ was observed, even though there were a number of **(4)** (n.) _____ who had been invited as guests. This was a time of celebration—a time to **(5)** (v.) _____ honors on those who had made the building of a world-class submarine possible, as well as to the **(6)** (n.) _____ of local community members and dignitaries who had provided financial support for the evening.

Most people in attendance were aware of being **(7)** (v.) _____ in the midst of local and national leaders in making the event a reality. Because of their hard work, everyone felt the **(8)** (n.) _____ of a strong kinship, satisfaction, and pride during the celebratory fireworks that provided a brief **(9)** (n.) _____ from the formality of after-dinner speeches. Although some critics **(10)** (v.) _____ at the expense of such an evening, others viewed it as a time to honor the ship's crew and extended family who would call the vessel home for the next few years.

Stop and Think

 Pyramid Summary: Choose two words from this chapter and complete the pyramid summaries below. You may consult your dictionary or go to **www.dictionary.reference.com** and **www.etymonline.com** for additional help. Then compare your pyramids with a partner.

    1. Word
    2. Synonym
    3. Antonym
    4. Etymology
    5. Sentence

            1. _____
          2. _____
       3. _____
     4. _____
  5. _____

            1. _____
          2. _____
       3. _____
     4. _____
  5. _____

Go to **www.suemorem.com** and click on "Tips." On your own paper, summarize a section of your choice on etiquette. Be sure to use the words *acknowledge, precise,* and *protocol* in the summary.

Vocabulary and Sociology of Marriage and Family

Get Ready to Read About Sociology of Marriage and Family

A college course on marriage and the family is a specialized sociology course in which students learn about the courtship, marriage, and family customs of a variety of cultures. Because the course is not limited to a national view, students gain a global perspective of these traditions. Before you read the selection, consider the word parts you already know and fill in the blanks.

1. The prefix *con-* means _____.

2. The prefix *ex-* means _____.

3. The prefix *per-* means *through*.

4. The prefix *poly-* means _____.

5. The prefix *re-* means _____.

6. The root *andro* means _____.

7. The root *gamy* means _____.

8. The root *gyn* means _____.

9. The root *spect* means _____.

10. The suffix *-fy* means *cause to become* and indicates a _____.

concept	exogamy	perspective	polygyny	specify
endogamy	norm	polyandry	regard	theme

MARRIAGE AND FAMILY IN GLOBAL PERSPECTIVE

To better understand U.S. patterns of marriage and family, let's first look at how customs differ around the world. This will give us a context for interpreting our own experiences in this vital social institution.

What Is a Family?

"What is a family, anyway?" asked William Sayres at the beginning of an article on this topic. By this question, he meant that although the family is so significant to humanity that it is universal—every human group in the world organizes its members in families—the world's cultures display so much variety that the term *family* is difficult to define. For example, although the Western world **regards** a family as a husband, wife, and children, other groups have family forms in which men have more than one wife (**polygyny**) or women more than one husband (**polyandry**). How about the obvious? Can we define family as the approved group into which children are born? This would overlook the Banaro of New Guinea. In this group, a young woman must give birth before she can marry—and she *cannot* marry the father of her child.

Common Cultural Themes

Despite this diversity, several common **themes** do run through the **concepts** of marriage and family. All societies use marriage and family to establish patterns of mate selection, descent, inheritance, and authority. Let's look at these patterns.

Mate Selection. Each human group establishes **norms** to govern who marries whom. Norms of **endogamy** specify that people should marry within their own group. Groups may prohibit interracial marriages, for example. In contrast, norms of **exogamy specify** that people must marry outside their group.

—From James M. Henslin, *Essentials of Sociology*, 5e, pp. 324-326. Published by Allyn and Bacon, Boston, MA. Copyright © 2004 by Pearson Education. Reprinted by permission of the publisher.

VISUAL VOCABULARY

A devoted father teaches his

_____ of life to his son, and he hopes his view of the world will guide him.

a. norm
b. perspective

Courtesy of Microsoft.

EXERCISE 1 Context Clues

Refer to the previous passage and use context clues from the sentences below to determine the definition of each of the following words in **bold** print. Do not consult a dictionary.

1. concept (kŏn′sĕpt′) n.
According to psychologist Lawrence Kohlberg, individuals develop a **concept** of right and wrong as they move through six stages of moral development.

_____ **Concept** means
    a. fantasy.   c. fictional interpretation.
    b. idea.   d. denial.

2. endogamy (ĕn-dŏg′ə-mē) n.
Naomi's family is from India and practices **endogamy**, which means that she must someday marry a man with a background similar to hers.

_____ **Endogamy** means
    a. marriage within a group.   c. marrying more than one spouse.
    b. marriage outside a group.   d. marrying more than one husband.

3. exogamy (ĕk-sŏg′ə-mē) n.
Although **exogamy** was not legal for many generations in the United States, interracial couples are now allowed to marry and such marriages are more prevalent worldwide.

_____ **Exogamy** means
    a. marriage within a group.   c. marrying more than one spouse.
    b. marriage outside a group.   d. marrying more than one husband.

4. norm (nôrm) n.
Because he did not appear to be part of the **norm** with his green hair and body piercings, Alex realized he would have to dress more conservatively when he began job hunting.

_____ **Norm** means
    a. exception.   c. extreme standard.
    b. average standard.   d. unusual standard.

5. perspective (pər-spĕk′tĭv) n.
Whenever Emily begins to feel discouraged, she gets a new **perspective** on her own problems by volunteering at a local soup kitchen.

_____ **Perspective** means
    a. command.   c. decline.
    b. volunteer.   d. view.

6. polyandry (pŏl′ē-ăn′drē) n.
"I think our government should allow **polyandry**," quipped Shar, "because a woman needs three husbands: one to go to work, one to do jobs around the house, and one to escort her to formal affairs."

_____ **Polyandry** means
    a. practice of having more than one spouse.
    b. practice of having more than one wife.
    c. practice of having more than one husband.
    d. practice of remaining unmarried.

7. polygyny (pə-lĭg′-ə-nē) n.
Islam allows **polygyny**; that is, a man is allowed to have up to four wives as long as he can provide equally for each wife, both financially and emotionally.

_____ **Polygyny** means
   a. practice of having more than one spouse.
   b. practice of having more than one wife.
   c. practice of having more than one husband.
   d. practice of remaining unmarried.

8. regard (rĭ-gärd′) v.

Some people **regard** their jobs as their sole purpose and total identity; however, they need to find balance in their lives and fulfillment in their relationships in order to make good memories.

_____ **Regard** means
   a. consider.   c. avoid.
   b. ignore.   d. excuse.

9. specify (spĕs′ə-fī′) v.

When Tyler asked his supervisor for a raise, he was prepared to **specify** reasons he deserved more money.

_____ **Specify** means
   a. condense.   c. cite.
   b. mistake.   d. confuse.

10. theme (thēm) n.

The novels of Robert B. Parker usually center on the **themes** of self-reliance and autonomy, teaching readers about the need to become independent.

_____ **Theme** means
   a. song.   c. entertainment park.
   b. key idea.   d. arrangement.

EXERCISE **2** Word Sorts

Synonyms

Match the word to the synonyms or definitions that follow each blank.

1. _____ the practice of having more than one wife at a time

2. _____ attend; consider; look at; view

3. _____ thesis; subject; thought; premise

4. _____ idea; perception; belief; notion

5. _____ viewpoint; angle; attitude; standpoint

Antonyms

Select the letter of the word(s) with the opposite meaning.

_____ **6.** polyandry
   a. marrying outside the tribe   c. having one husband
   b. having one wife   d. having several husbands

_____ **7.** endogamy
   a. having several wives
   b. marrying within one's group
   c. having several husbands
   d. marrying outside one's group

_____ **8.** exogamy
   a. marrying within one's group   c. having many wives
   b. marrying outside one's group   d. having many husbands

_____ **9.** norm
   a. custom   c. model
   b. average   d. exception

_____ **10.** specify
   a. define   c. acknowledge
   b. ignore   d. allow

EXERCISE **3** Fill in the Blank

Use context clues to determine the word that best completes each sentence.

1. Mountain hiking always provides me with a new _____ by offering an expansive view of my surroundings and making the difficult things in life seem less important.

2. Mr. Smith _____ each employee as valuable, and he finds frequent opportunities to express his appreciation.

3. The _____ of global warming is not a possibility some people want to consider.

4. One trait that many cults seem to share is discouraging _____, because they believe married couples should share the same beliefs.

5. Before we signed the contract, we insisted on reading the fine print, and we asked the salesperson to _____ the details of the warranty.

6. At an outdoor concert based on the _____ of children's fairy tales, Paul proposed to his girlfriend during the grand finale, which featured music from *Cinderella*.

7. Occasionally being unpredictable and doing something out of the _____ will give you a break from a boring routine.

8. Sarah's father had always expected that she would honor his rules of _____ and marry a man from the Greek Orthodox Church; however, when he met her new boyfriend Josh, a Roman Catholic, he was pleased with her choice.

9. Although the practice of marrying more than one wife simultaneously has been publicized about some cultures, we rarely hear of cultures that allow _____, in which a woman is legally married to more than one man.

10. No matter how hard they try, Lydia's girlfriends could not understand how the five wives of a man in Utah could allow the conditions of _____ and share the same husband.

EXERCISE 4 Application

Using context clues, insert the vocabulary word in the appropriate blank. A part-of-speech clue is given for each vocabulary word.

Before each lesson, our sociology professor requires us to write a double-entry journal. The assignment is to write 150–250 words about a **(1)** (n.) _____ we are going to study. Since we have an established **(2)** (n.) _____ for the journal entry, we draw on our own background knowledge in order to make connections with our reading. Recently, our professor posed some interesting questions: "What do you **(3)** (v.) _____ as a family?" and "**(4)** (v.) _____ what qualities you consider necessary for a true marriage."

Later in his lecture, our professor prompted a discussion about the practice of **(5)** (n.) _____, in which couples in some countries are forbidden to marry someone outside the tribe or religious group. Naturally, this idea was foreign to us until he reminded the class about some dating and marriage laws in our own country before the civil rights movement of the 1960s, the play of *Romeo and Juliet*, and the film *West Side Story* that presented the tragic romance of Tony and Maria. In all of these cases, the lesson was always that **(6)** (n.) _____ was the practice of star-crossed lovers who eventually would meet with disaster.

At that point, our professor asked about **(7)** (n.) _____ (the practice of taking more than one husband) and **(8)** (n.) _____ (the practice of taking more than one wife). When we all agreed the ideas were very odd, he suggested that we consider serial polygamy, which, from the **(9)** (n.) _____ of people in other countries, occurs in the United States whenever couples divorce, remarry, divorce a second time, and then remarry yet another spouse. This new view gave us something to think about. Suddenly, what may be the **(10)** (n.) _____ to famous celebrities with shaky marriages in our country seemed similar to the typical practice of having several spouses in another country. The lesson was a powerful one in helping us develop a global view, and it enabled us to appreciate how we are all actually more alike than different.

Stop and Think

Using at least three words from the vocabulary list, summarize the sociology passage at the beginning of the chapter in 50 words or less in the space below.

_____

_____

_____

_____

_____

_____

Consult your dictionary, **www.dictionary.com**, and **www.etymonline** to determine 20 words and their definitions with the prefix *poly-*. (Answers will vary, but examples are included below.)

1. _____

2. _____

3. _____

4. _____

5. _____

6. _____

7. _____

8. _____

9. _____

10. _____

11. _____

12. _____

13. _____

14. _____

15. _____

_____

16. _____

17. _____

18. _____

19. _____

20. _____

Vocabulary and Psychology

Get Ready to Read About Psychology

Psychology is the study of mental processes and behavior. The word *psychology* comes from the root *psych*, which means *mind,* and the suffix *–ology*, which means *study of*. As you read about psychology, you will make connections to your own experiences, and you will grow to understand yourself and others better. Before you read the selection, consider the word parts you already know and fill in the blanks.

1. The prefix *re-* means *again.*

2. The root *ultima* means *final.*

3. The suffix *-ity* means _____, and indicates a _____.

4. The suffix *-ical* means _____, and indicates an _____.

5. The suffix *-or* means _____, and indicates a _____.

adversity	harness	moral	psychological	stimulus
chemotherapy	impending	process	sheer	ultimately

SENSATION AND PERCEPTION

A picture of Tour de France winner Lance Armstrong hangs on my bulletin board. I look at the photo every day and it gives me a bit of inspiration.

Some days I'm inspired because of his **sheer** talent as an athlete (something that I'm not); other days, it's because at a young age Armstrong learned a valuable lesson about life (that it's not about winning); and other days I think about his ability to withstand pain and **adversity** in his illness (cancer) and his bike rides (the longest and toughest known). Lance—I call him Lance—used **psychological** processes to overcome difficulties of **chemotherapy,** surgery, and the punishing pain of the Tour de France. Most people know that pain is a signal of damage to the body or **impending** damage, but Lance was able to turn it off, endure it, and overcome—it was a matter of mind over body. Lance Armstrong's achievements are not only ones of **moral** courage, but they are psychological ones as well that show that one's situation, culture, family background, and **ultimately** one's belief all affect the ability to experience, endure, and in some cases, overcome pain. (You might want to read Lance's autobiography, *It's Not About the Bike* (2000), if you'd like to see how to **harness** some of the techniques he used in times of adversity and competition.)

Psychologists are interested in pain because it involves one of the five senses, because it helps us understand the human condition, and because it is a model of how human beings **process** information—from a sharp **stimulus**, to the receptors, and to experiences. Psychologists pay particular attention to the beginnings and ends of the process—either from the stimulus (such as a sharp object) or the response (the pain that is felt) on how they record information.

–From Lester A. Lefton and Linda Brannon, *Psychology,* 8e, pp. 143-145. Published by Allyn and Bacon, Boston, MA. Copyright © 2003 by Pearson Education. Reprinted by permission of the publisher.

VISUAL VOCABULARY

With a(n) _____ storm, a windmill can harness more power from nature.

   a. impending
   b. moral

Courtesy of Microsoft.

EXERCISE **1** Context Clues

Refer to the previous passage and use context clues from the sentences below to determine the definition of each of the following words in **bold** print. Do not consult a dictionary.

1. adversity (ăd-vûr′sĭ-tē) n.
   Our courage is tested and strengthened when we are thrust into **adversity** and forced to face difficult trials.

   _____ **Adversity** means
   a. improvement.   c. good fortune.
   b. service.   d. hardship.

2. chemotherapy (kē′mō-thĕr′ə-pē) n.
   Many new forms of **chemotherapy** are less brutal on a patient and more successful than ever in destroying cancer cells.

   _____ **Chemotherapy** means
   a. drug cancer treatment.   c. success.
   b. herbal remedy.   d. alternative medicine.

3. harness (här′nĭs) v.
   Because of diminishing oil supplies, energy companies are researching ways to **harness** solar and wind power.

   _____ **Harness** means
   a. release.   c. eliminate.
   b. control.   d. expel.

4. impending (ĭm-pĕnd-ŋ) adj.
   Instead of waiting until the night before an **impending** exam, students should begin studying after the first day of class.

   _____ **Impending** means
   a. distant.   c. forthcoming.
   b. past.   d. opposing.

5. moral (môr′əl) adj.
   Cloning presents a **moral** dilemma because although the procedure may eliminate some serious disease, critics say it could be at the expense of a human life.

   _____ **Moral** means
   a. having a sense of right and wrong.   c. satisfying.
   b. showing physical strength.   d. having a sense of foolishness.

6. process (prŏs′ĕs′) v.

"I eat almonds for a snack," said John, "because they help the receptors in my brain to **process** information more efficiently, which then improves my memory."

_____ **Process** means

a. undermine.
b. deal with.

c. need.
d. destroy.

7. psychological (sī′kə-lŏj′-kəl) adj.

Many returning soldiers confess that in spite of their survival training, they have suffered some **psychological** difficulties as a result of the war.

_____ **Psychological** means

a. having to do with the mind.
b. having to do with the physical body.

c. having to do with business.
d. having to do with education.

8. sheer (shîr) adj.

While driving in the Southwest, we were amazed by the **sheer** expanse of land and the distant horizon that seemed to grow.

_____ **Sheer** means

a. see through.
b. absolute; total.

c. unnoticeable.
d. expected.

9. stimulus (stĭm′yə-ləs) n.

Using doggie treats as a **stimulus** to train Honey, her golden retriever, Kat was able to teach the dog several new tricks.

_____ **Stimulus** means

a. discouragement.
b. motivator.

c. sympathy.
d. reaction.

10. ultimately (ŭl′tə-mĭt-lē) adv.

Although he initially fought the temptation, Jared **ultimately** left his books in the library and followed the sounds of cheering at the football stadium.

_____ **Ultimately** means

a. never.
b. first.

c. eventually.
d. casually.

EXERCISE 2 Word Sorts

Synonyms

Match the word to the synonyms or definitions that follow each blank.

1. _____ boost; incentive; cause

2. _____ cancer treatment using certain chemicals to destroy malignant cells

3. _____ relating to the mind or emotions

4. _____ deal with; handle; make ready; prepare

5. _____ altogether; absolute; total; complete

Antonyms

Select the letter of the word(s) with the opposite meaning.

_____ 6. ultimately
   a. last   b. never   c. final   d. daily

_____ 7. moral
   a. good   b. evil   c. blameless   d. high-minded

_____ 8. adversity
   a. work   b. hardship   c. bad luck   d. good fortune

_____ 9. harness
   a. favor   b. control   c. limit   d. release

_____ 10. impending
   a. past   b. approaching c. near   d. forthcoming

EXERCISE 3 Fill in the Blank

Use context clues to determine the word that best completes each sentence.

1. Molly confessed that she was under a great deal of stress because her boss,

   a man who was completely focused on his _____ promotion, had become a bundle of nerves.

2. If you suffer from sleep deprivation, you'll discover that the receptors in your brain will function less efficiently, making it difficult to

   _____ new information.

3. When I see active children, I wish I could _____ their energy and joy and give it to those people who cannot motivate themselves to be productive.

4. No matter what excuse we give, our success in college _____ depends on our own self-discipline and determination.

5. Early childhood experts agree that the _____ benefits of reading aloud to children are numerous, including the promotion of language skills and self-discipline as well as the presentation of learning as a pleasant experience.

6. When he was considering his own _____, Frederick Douglass wrote, "Without a struggle, there can be no progress."

7. A good teacher or coach can be the _____ that causes young people to work hard and accomplish more than they thought they were capable of doing.

8. Adam was surprised by the _____ volume of reading and writing required in his freshman classes.

9. Although the *Chronicles of Narnia* by C. S. Lewis are great adventure stories,

   they are also books with _____ themes presenting battles between good and evil.

10. After several bouts of _____, Wade received the good news from his oncologist that his leukemia was in remission.

EXERCISE **4** Application

Using context clues, insert the vocabulary word in the appropriate blank. A part-of-speech clue is given for each vocabulary word.

Shelly had always been the picture of health. Yet, when she received the news from her doctor that her test results indicated she had cancer, she was immediately overwhelmed with fear at the thought of the **(1)** (adj.) _____ surgery and follow-up treatments. Cancer treatments can be frightening at first; however, education is often the key that helps us **(2)** (v.) _____ the fear and **(3)** (v.) _____ that energy into a positive outlook in order to be victorious. A good support system is also important in overcoming any **(4)** (n.) _____, and research indicates that a network of family and friends can be instrumental in easing the difficulty and pain of **(5)** (n.) _____ and radiation treatments that often follow surgery.

The **(6)** (n.) _____ of a smile, a gentle touch, or a greeting card can also boost the immune system. Surprise gifts work, too! For Shelly that surprise came in the form of a huge basket filled with fragrant candles and soaps, CDs of soothing music, herbal teas, and dark chocolate—all gifts aimed at creating the **(7)** (adj.) _____ effects of comfort and healing.

And it worked. The **(8)** (adj.) _____ number of letters, e-mails, and phone messages lifted her spirits. **(9)** (adv.) _____, she was able to overcome her anxiety and her cancer. Now that she has been free of cancer for more than five years, she counsels those who have been newly diagnosed. "How can you do that?" a friend recently asked.

Shelly explained that it was her **(10)** (adj.) _____ responsibility to extend hope to others. "I have learned," Shelly said, "that we are all connected on this life journey. None of us can travel it alone if we hope to travel it well."

Stop and Think

Using at least three words from the list, summarize the passage in 50 words or less in the space below.

_____

_____

_____

Go to Lance Armstrong's Website at **http://www.lancearmstrong.com/** and view the photograph mentioned in the selection. Also, read his story as well as other stories of cancer survivorship. On your own paper, share your thoughts about overcoming adversity.

Vocabulary and American History

Get Ready to Read About American History

In a college student's curriculum, one of the general education requirements often includes a history course. An American history course includes some history as well as a study of current events. As you prepare to read the following selection, consider what you already know about immigration and the history of the United States, and connect that knowledge to recent news articles you have read about immigration. Finally, consider what you already know about the following word parts. The meanings of some have been provided. Recall what you learned in Chapter 1 and fill in the blanks for the others.

1. The prefix *in-* means *in, into, on.*

2. The prefix *multi-* means _____.

3. The root *flux* means _____.

4. The root *gen* means *race, kind, sex.*

5. The suffix *-ate* means *make* and usually indicates a _____.

6. The suffix *-ous* means *of, like, related to, being* and usually indicates an

   _____.

assimilate	heritage	influx	multilingual	surpass
attainment	indigenous	median	regardless	whereas

A NEW CLASS OF PROFESSIONAL WORKERS

Unlike Hispanics who have come to America to escape poverty, the recent **influx** of Asians has been driven by a new class of professional workers looking for greater opportunity. As Ronald Takaki documents, Asians who have come to America since the 1965 Immigration Act opened the gate to them make up the most highly skilled immigrant group in American history. Indeed, Asian Americans have often been called the superachievers of the minority majority. This is especially true in the case of educational **attainment**—42 percent of Asian Americans over the age of 25 hold a college degree, almost twice the national average. As a result, their **median** family income has already **surpassed** that of non-Hispanic whites.

Whereas Asian Americans are the best off of America's minority groups, by far the worst off is the one **indigenous** minority, known today as Native Americans. Before Europeans arrived in America, 12 to 15 million Native Americans lived here. War and disease reduced their numbers to a mere 210,000 by 1910. About 1.8 million Americans currently list themselves as being of Native American **heritage.** Statistics show that they are the least healthy, the poorest, and the least educated group in the American melting pot. Only a handful of Native Americans have found wealth; fewer still have any power. Some tribes have discovered oil or other minerals on their land and have used these resources successfully. Most Native Americans, though, remain economically and politically disadvantaged in American society. The 1990 census found that in the Dakotas, site of the largest Sioux reservations, over half of the Native Americans lived below the poverty line.

Americans live in an increasingly multicultural and **multilingual** society. Yet, **regardless** of ethnic background most Americans share a common political culture—an overall set of values widely shared within a society. For example, there is much agreement among ethnic groups about what truly makes an American. Minority groups have **assimilated** many basic American values, such as the principle of treating all equally.

—Adapted from *Government in America,* 9th Edition, by George C. Edwards III, Martin P. Wattenberg, and Robert L. Lineberry. New York: Longman, 2000, pp. 185-186. Reprinted by permission of Pearson Education, Inc., Glenview, IL.

VISUAL VOCABULARY

Native Americans have a proud

_____ and an important story to tell about that legacy.

  a. attainment
  b. heritage

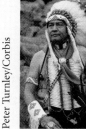

EXERCISE 1 Context Clues

Refer to the previous passage and use context clues from the sentences below to determine the definition of each of the following words in **bold** print. Do not consult a dictionary.

1. assimilate (ə-sĭm′ə-lāt′) v.
The students in each incoming freshman class experience a week of orientation so they can **assimilate** into the routines and traditions of the college.

    _____ **Assimilate** means
      a. blend.   c. surround with beautiful objects.
      b. study.   d. long for the past.

2. attainment (ə-tān′mənt) n.
The young CEO credited the successful **attainment** of his professional goals to his education in a one-room school in a West Virginia mining camp, explaining, "I had sixth grade six times, which gave me a strong foundation in reading, writing, arithmetic, and geography."

    _____ **Attainment** means
      a. laziness.   c. achievement.
      b. civilization.   d. cooperation.

3. heritage (hĕr′ĭ-tĭj) n.
"The **heritage** we leave to future generations will be long lines at the gas pumps if we do not find alternatives to foreign oil," argued the senator.

    _____ **Heritage** means
      a. partnership.   c. alternative.
      b. inheritance.   d. argument.

4. indigenous (ĭn-dĭj′ə-nəs) adj.
The Dreamtime of the Aborigines is one of the fascinating features of the **indigenous** people of the Australian Outback.

_____ **Indigenous** means
    a. unusual.   c. unfamiliar.
    b. native.   d. abnormal.

5. influx (ĭn′flŭks′) n.
The **influx** of new students each fall creates an exciting atmosphere for everyone involved in the college experience.

_____ **Influx** means
    a. mass arrival.   c. boredom.
    b. mass exit.   d. disappointment.

6. median (mē′dē-ən) n.
The **median** income in America exceeds that of the average income of most families worldwide.

_____ **Median** means
    a. taxed.   c. famous.
    b. profession.   d. middle.

7. multilingual (mŭl′tē-lĭng′gwəl) adj.
Some Fortune 500 companies have become so competitive that they require new employees to be **multilingual**; that is, they want their employees to speak several languages in order to function in a global market.

_____ **Multilingual** means
    a. able to speak a foreign language.   c. able to use good grammar.
    b. able to speak several foreign languages.   d. able to be a good public speaker.

8. regardless (rĭ-gärd′lĭs) adv.
Because Madison's mother insisted that the wedding reception take place outside **regardless** of the forecast, the wedding planner arranged for an enclosed, air-conditioned tent with a wooden dance floor.

_____ **Regardless** means
    a. in spite of.   c. without.
    b. during.   d. because of.

9. surpass (sər-păs′) v.
The life coach explained that eliminating clutter helps her clients organize their lives, thus providing more time and energy to help them quickly **surpass** their goals.

_____ **Surpass** means
    a. prevent.   c. go beyond.
    b. suggest.   d. eliminate.

10. whereas (hwâr-ăz′) conj.
Jerome has a tendency to make excuses, skip class, and turn in poor quality work, **whereas** Andy attends regularly, studies beyond the assigned readings, and turns in excellent projects.

_____ **Whereas** means
    a. because.   c. then.
    b. on the other hand.   d. as a result.

EXERCISE 2 Word Sorts

Synonyms

Match the word to the synonyms or definitions that follow each blank.

1. _____ birthright; legacy; inheritance; ancestry

2. _____ average; middle; midway; central

3. _____ despite; in contrast; conversely; in spite of

4. _____ characterized by the ability to speak several languages

5. _____ reaching; achieving; acquiring; succeeding

Antonyms

Select the letter of the word(s) with the opposite meaning.

_____ **6.** surpass: a. exceed b. transcend c. rise d. drop behind

_____ **7.** assimilate: a. blend b. stand out c. accompany d. go beyond

_____ **8.** indigenous: a. native b. complete c. natural d. foreign

_____ **9.** influx: a. mass entrance b. mass exit c. flood d. river

_____ **10.** whereas: a. although b. even though c. similarly d. despite

EXERCISE **3** Fill in the Blank

Use context clues to determine the word that best completes each sentence.

1. Ashley is athletic and outspoken, often writing letters to the editor, _____ her sister Stephanie is a quiet beauty contest winner who always smiles and never reveals her opinions.

2. Although the basketball team lost its first seven games, the coach inspired the players to _____ the initial predictions, and they eventually won enough games to earn a spot in the play-offs.

3. A fraternity is composed of men who are able to _____ into the group because they share common traits and interests.

4. After the _____ of a promotion and a raise, the public relations executive surprised everyone by resigning from her job and signing on for two years in the Peace Corps.

5. After there was a sudden _____ of vultures, county animal control officials used air horns for several days, and the annoying birds exited permanently.

6. Our Night-blooming Cereus, a tree-dwelling cactus that is _____ to the West Indies, has fascinated many visitors over the years who come to see the beautiful and fragrant white blossoms that only last one night.

7. The local Native American tribes have protested the state's plans to create a new reservoir using land that has been part of their _____ since colonial times.

8. After her college courses and study-abroad experience, Dana will be _____, comfortably speaking Italian, French, and Spanish.

9. The _____ age of people in our community has decreased over the years from 37 to 25.

10. "_____ of your excuse, you are still required to make up the test on the day you return to class," explained our physics professor on the first day of class.

EXERCISE **4** Application

Using context clues, insert the vocabulary word in the appropriate blank. A part-of-speech clue is given for each vocabulary word.

Native Americans, those people **(1)** (adj.) _____ to the country, have a proud **(2)** (n.) _____ that deserves serious reflection. **(3)** (adv.) _____ of few appearances in print and film, Native Americans, the oldest minority, currently have a population of two million. Many are **(4)** (adj.) _____, preserving the language of several tribes as well as speaking English. Unfortunately, their history has been filled with discrimination and exploitation since the **(5)** (n.) _____ of Europeans in the 17th century. Consequently, some Native Americans remain isolated. Others, however, have left the reservation and learned to **(6)** (v.) _____ and blend with those outside the tribe. They have become well known in many areas. For example, the words of Black Hawk and Black Elk are studied today, in addition to the literature of Scott Momaday. Likewise, an industry promoting their art and music has **(7)** (v.) _____ original expectations, becoming very profitable.

(8) (conj.) _____ some Native Americans are experiencing progress, many more continue to suffer educationally and economically. For example, the **(9)** (adj.) _____ income of most remains below the poverty level and the **(10)** (n.) _____ of a better life seems out of their reach. Yet, it is not impossible if we remember the words of Lone Man (Isna-la-wica) Teton Sioux, who said, "I have seen that in any great undertaking it is not enough for a man to depend simply upon himself." Thus, the struggle of one becomes the struggle of many.

Stop and Think

  Connect a word from the chapter to the picture, and then write your rationale.

Courtesy of Microsoft.	1._____ _____ _____
Courtesy of Microsoft.	2._____ _____
Courtesy of Microsoft.	3._____ _____ _____
Courtesy of Microsoft.	4._____ _____
Courtesy of Microsoft.	5._____ _____ _____

  Go to the National Museum of the American Indian at **http://www.nmai.si.edu** and explore the site. On your own paper, in 150 words, describe what you have discovered. Include the words *indigenous* and *heritage*.

12

Vocabulary and American Government

Get Ready to Read About American Government

Most college students have some background knowledge in government if the subject was a high school graduation requirement. Consequently, college students often elect to take a course in United States government or national politics because of their background knowledge.

Before you read, review the word parts below. The meanings of some have been provided. Recall what you learned in Chapter 1 and fill in the blanks for the others.

1. The prefix *con-* means _____.

2. The prefix *im-* means _____.

3. The root *ven* means _____.

4. The root *sonare* means *to sound*.

5. The suffix *-ous* means *of, like, related to, full of* and indicates an

_____.

6. The suffix *-tion* means *act* or *state* and indicates a _____.

cadence	convention	instigation	quip	sonorous
constitute	flout	lampoon	ruefully	stodgy

KENNEDY'S CAMELOT

Having **lampooned** the Eisenhower administration as **stodgy** and unimaginative, President Kennedy made a show of his style and wit. He **flouted convention** by naming his younger brother Robert attorney general. "I can't see that it's wrong to give him a little legal experience before he goes out to practice law," the president **quipped**. Kennedy also prided himself on being a man of letters, winner of the Pulitzer Prize for *Profiles in Courage.* He quoted Robert Frost and Dante. He played and replayed recordings of Winston Churchill, hoping to imprint the great orator's **sonorous cadences** on his own flat Bostonian vowels. At the **instigation** of his elegant wife, Jacqueline, Kennedy surrounded himself with the finest intellects at glittering White House galas to honor Nobel Prize winners and celebrated artists.

Kennedy's youthful senior staff boasted impressive scholarly credentials. His national security advisor, McGeorge Bundy, had been dean of the faculty at Harvard (and the first undergraduate at Yale to receive perfect scores in three college entrance examinations). Secretary of Defense Robert McNamara also had taught at Harvard before becoming the first non-family member to head the Ford Motor Company. The administration **constituted,** as journalist David Halberstam observed later, somewhat **ruefully**, "the best and the brightest."

—From Mark C. Carnes and John A. Garraty, *The American Nation,* 11th Edition. New York: Longman, 2003, p. 789. Reprinted by permission of Pearson Education, Inc., Glenview, IL.

VISUAL VOCABULARY

When practicing, athletes often create a _____ to help them keep a rhythm and fast pace going as a team.

a. cadence
b. convention

Courtesy of Microsoft.

EXERCISE **1** Context Clues

Refer to the previous passage and use context clues from the sentences below to determine the definition of each of the following words in **bold** print. Do not consult a dictionary.

1. cadence (kād′ns) n.
   To memorize the sequence of events leading up to World War I, our study group created a "call out" by putting the events to a **cadence** and then repeating them while we jogged on the treadmill together at the gym.

   _____ **Cadence** means
       a. rhythm.   c. group.
       b. improvement.   d. exercise.

2. constitute (kŏn′stĭ-tōōt′) v.
   In her essay, Amy wrote that four characteristics **constitute** a good leader: honesty, vision, a strong work ethic, and a willingness to do whatever he or she asks of others.

   _____ **Constitute** means
       a. to question.   c. make up.
       b. discuss.   d. to lead.

3. convention (kən-věn′shən) n.
   Our instructor ignores the **conventions** of typical lectures and instead keeps us interested by using a variety of unusual teaching methods.

   _____ **Convention** means
       a. exciting example.   c. unusual technique.
       b. interesting gathering. d. traditional practice.

4. flout (flout) v.
   Jack **flouted** all warnings about climbing the cliff and nearly fell from a dangerous height.

   _____ **Flout** means
       a. apologize.   c. take seriously.
       b. laugh at.   d. agree.

5. instigation (ĭn′stĭ-gā-shən) n.
   Although Greg had planned to major in business, he changed his mind at the **instigation** of his advisor, who kept pointing out Greg's talent for history as well as some job opportunities in a field that he had not considered.

_____ **Instigation** means

a. consequence.

b. effect.

c. motivation.

d. answer.

6. lampoon (lăm-po͞on) v.

During a recent appearance in New York, former U.S. Poet Laureate Billy Collins read his humorous poem that **lampoons** the true thoughts of a dog about its master.

_____ **Lampoon** means

a. mock.

b. praise.

c. compliment.

d. prove.

7. quip (kwĭp) v.

In response to the student who asked if he had missed anything while he was absent, the professor **quipped,** "No, we all sat around with our hands folded waiting for your return."

_____ **Quip** means

a. consider seriously.

b. solve.

c. educate.

d. joke.

8. ruefully (ro͞o′fəl-lē) adv.

After her visit with him in California, Brittany **ruefully** admitted to Jason that he was a wonderful person, but he would always just be her very good friend.

_____ **Ruefully** means

a. sorrowfully.

b. happily.

c. energetically.

d. studiously.

9. sonorous (sŏn′ər-əs) adj.

Because of his excellent communication skills and **sonorous** speaking style, Anthony was encouraged to pursue a degree in broadcast journalism.

_____ **Sonorous** means

a. having a full, rich sound.

b. offensive.

c. boring.

d. having inaccurate details.

10. stodgy (stŏj′ē) adj.

Our geology professor looked like a **stodgy,** worn-out man; however, we were delighted to discover that he was actually an interesting, intelligent, and entertaining teacher.

_____ **Stodgy** means

a. youthful.

b. lively.

c. exciting.

d. dull.

EXERCISE **2** Word Sorts

Synonyms

Match the word to the synonyms or definitions that follow each blank.

1. _____ deep; resonant; deep-toned

2. _____ sorrowfully; regretfully; apologetically; compassionately

3. _____ defy; disregard; resist; contravene

4. _____ rhythm; beat; count; tempo

5. _____ ridicule; satirize; parody

Antonyms

Select the letter of the word(s) with the opposite meaning.

_____ **6.** constitute
    a. form   b. abolish   c. represent   d. surround

_____ **7.** quip
    a. ridicule   b. argue   c. mock   d. insult

_____ **8.** instigation
    a. discouragement   b. encouragement   c. attention   d. hard work

_____ **9.** convention
    a. practice   b. custom   c. exception   d. transaction

_____ **10.** stodgy
    a. stuffy   b. tasteless   c. exciting   d. dull

EXERCISE **3** Fill in the Blank

Use context clues to determine the vocabulary word that best completes each sentence.

1. In some states, Photo Red, the stoplight system with cameras installed, is used to detect the drivers who _____ the rules and drive through red lights.

2. With each new election, it seems a comedian surfaces who can _____ the current president, making fun of his mannerisms, his verbal mistakes, and his policies.

3. According to some psychologists, students may find their study sessions will be more effective if they play instrumental background music with a

_____ of 50 beats per minute.

4. When the college president announced his retirement, we

_____ began to imagine how different the campus would be without him and immediately felt sad about the loss.

5. With the _____ of his adventurous cousin, Alan decided to purchase an old sailboat and sail solo along the coast before starting college.

6. Carlos accepted his _____ uncle's invitation to visit Las Vegas with some concerns; however, he quickly discovered that his mother's brother was actually a very fun-loving and generous man.

7. The _____ voice and eloquent speech of the graduation speaker inspired the audience to give him a standing ovation.

8. Schooled in the _____ of etiquette, our friend Spencer helped us through the formal dinner at the college president's home, so that we were all able to feel at ease.

9. George explained that grilled salmon, baked potatoes, salad, and Dutch

oven cake _____ the perfect campfire dinner.

10. Whenever one of my professors is asked what subject he teaches, he

_____ "I do not teach a subject, I teach people."

EXERCISE 4 Application

Using context clues, insert the vocabulary word in the appropriate blank. A part-of-speech clue is given for each vocabulary word.

When Megan arrived on campus her freshman year, she immed-

iately experienced some anxiety. The tall stone buildings that

(1) (v.) _____ the main part of the old campus were impressive

as well as frightening. The sound of the ROTC drill team marching to the

(2) (n.) _____ of their leader echoed through the walkways.

She thought back to the visit a year ago that had imprinted the image of this

place as the school she wanted to call home for four years. That weekend, she had listened to the **(3)** (adj.) _____ administrator, but also to the enthusiastic professor who lectured in a **(4)** (adj.) _____ and moving tone that inspired her to work hard and earn a spot in the freshman class.

If it had not been for the **(5)** (n.) _____ of her grandfather's confidence, Megan might never have summoned the courage to apply to a university with such an impressive reputation. In fact, **(6)** (n.) _____ dictated that she should apply to a school that was more associated with females rather than this male-dominated institution that specialized in math and engineering. Because she believed that a science-related career was her destiny, she **(7)** (v.) _____ the criticism of her classmates. Even today she will **(8)** (v.) _____, "No one asked me to be perfect—only to strive for perfection."

Although her high school friends **(9)** (v.) _____ her for having such high ambitions, they quickly changed their attitudes and **(10)** (adv.) _____ apologized when they discovered she had been accepted on early decision.

Stop and Think

 Study the photograph below and write a caption that uses one of the vocabulary words from the chapter.

_____
_____
_____
_____
_____
_____
_____

Elizabeth Pongratz

Go to **www.etymonline.com** to study the history of the following words. Then complete the summaries by filling in the blanks.

1. Cadence

The word appeared around _____ from the Middle French and meant _____ The Old Italian use of _____ meant "conclusion of a movement in music," or more literally "a falling," which evolved from the Latin word _____, which means _____

2. Flout

The word probably first appeared in _____ as a special use of the Middle English word *flowten,* which means _____. This form evolved from the Middle Dutch, *fluyten,* which meant "to play the flute" and _____ which also means "to make fun of."

3. Lampoon

Originally used in _____ from the French word *lampon,* it may be from _____, which means "let us drink." This word often appeared in irreverent 17th century _____. It is also connected to the word _____, which meant "to guzzle."

4. Rue

The verb is from the Old English *hreowan,* which means _____ and blended with the verb *hreowian,* meaning "feel pain or sorrow." As a noun, *rue* appeared in _____ in reference to an evergreen shrub whose leaves left a _____.

5. Sonorous

In _____, the word evolved from the Latin *sonorous,* meaning _____ and from *sonor,* which means _____.

Review Test
Chapters 8-12

1 Word Parts

Match the definitions in Column 2 to the word parts in Column 1.

Column 1		Column 2
_____	**1.** gamy	a. below
_____	**2.** poly-	b. forward; for
_____	**3.** sub-	c. male; man
_____	**4.** gyn	d. look; watch
_____	**5.** spec	e. many
_____	**6.** psych	f. marriage
_____	**7.** end-	g. within
_____	**8.** gen	h. female; woman
_____	**9.** andro	i. mind
_____	**10.** pro-	j. race; kind; sex

1   **2 Fill in the Blank**

Use context clues to determine the best word from the box to complete each sentence.

adversity	endogamy	harness	psychological	surpass
civilian	exogamy	polyandry	regardless	whereas

1. After months of training, Stephen _____ his own expectations in the 10K run when he finished with a time of 32 minutes and 12 seconds.

2. Whereas it is fairly common to find countries that allow men to marry several wives, it is much harder to find a community where women practice _____.

3. After serving a long career in the military and retiring as a colonel, Chris looked forward to life as a _____ when he took a job with a private contractor.

4. Although lack of poverty is not an _____, Dr. Ben Carson believes that being rich presents a different kind of obstacle for his three sons.

5. Joanne is planning to move to the mountains to begin a residency at a hospital, _____ her boyfriend Brian will remain in the city and continue working on his graduate degree.

6. Ian, the army chaplain's assistant, views everyone with equal compassion, _____ of past behavior.

7. Allowing soldiers to go to war if they have some _____ issues can be harmful to everyone because their mental health can further deteriorate if they do not get some help.

8. Learning to _____ alternate forms of energy such as ethanol, biomass, wind, and even cooking grease will take creativity, but it could also reduce our need for foreign oil.

9. Some countries still influence their young people to practice _____ because they do not welcome strangers from other tribes or countries into their community.

10. Speed dating was originally created by the Jewish community to encourage young people to meet partners of the same religion and to discourage _____, or marrying outside their faith.

3 Book Connection

Use context clues to determine the best word from the box to complete each sentence. A part-of-speech clue is given for each vocabulary word.

assimilate	constitute	indigenous	instigation	theme
concept	flout	influx	norm	ultimately

THE BEAN TREES

Writer Barbara Kingsolver found her "voice" when she learned that the first line of a book should begin with a promise that the author keeps throughout the story. Her novel *The Bean Trees* begins with just such a promise as she introduces the main character, Taylor Greer. A young girl from a small town in Kentucky, Taylor is not average. Instead of falling into the trap of becoming the **(1)** (n.) _____ in her town, which is a young, unwed mother who drops out of school, Taylor **(2)** (v.) _____ the lifestyle of her classmates and chooses another path instead. First, she finishes high school, and at the **(3)** (n.) _____ of her mother who gives her courage, she gets a job in a local hospital. After a few years of saving her money, she sets out on an adventure in an old VW Beetle, traveling across the country. For her, a better life is only a **(4)** (n.) _____ she believes in, but cannot imagine. Like Dorothy in *The Wizard of Oz*, however, she encounters people on her journey—people who help her find her way.

One of the **(5)** (n.) _____ of the book, in fact, is that of a journey, and the main character has also been compared to Huck Finn who travels the Mississippi River in search of answers.

3

In spite of her fear of tires blowing up, Taylor ends up in Tucson, Arizona, working at Jesus Is Lord Used Tires, which she first regards as something odd, not only because of the name, but also because of an **(6)** (n.) _____ of Latinos who arrive at the store and are soon quietly escorted to another location. She later learns they **(7)** (v.) _____ a population of illegal immigrants who are in search of safety.

As Taylor becomes **(8)** (v.) _____ into the life of her new home, which she believes is like a foreign land, she also raises Turtle, a three-year-old girl who was given to her while she traveled through an Indian reservation in Oklahoma. Together they delight in learning about the flowers and animals **(9)** (adj.) _____ to the desert, and they both flourish as beautifully as the wisteria vines whose seed pods make them look like bean trees. **(10)** (adv.) _____, Taylor and Turtle make a home for themselves while also helping people they encounter. But the story is not over. Barbara Kingsolver continues their tale in the sequel, *Pigs in Heaven*, presenting a new dilemma for the readers to consider.

4 Visual Connection

Write a caption for this picture using two of the words from the box.

attainment	median	process	ruefully	sneer
impending	precise	regard	sheer	sonorous

Courtsey of Microsoft.

_____

_____

_____

_____

_____

_____

5 Analogies

Choose the word that best completes the analogy.

1. serious : criticize :: funny: _____
   a. bestow   b. specify   c. lampoon

2. song : melody :: rhythm : _____
   a. stimulus   b. cadence   c. intensity

3. receive : inherit :: donate : _____
   a. bestow   b. lampoon   c. specify

4. announce : proclaim :: spell out : _____
   a. bestow   b. thrust   c. specify

5. effect : cause :: response : _____
   a. cadence   b. intensity   c. stimulus

6. muscle : strength :: light : _____
   a. intensity   b. stimulus   c. process

7. mourn : weep :: joke : _____
   a. specify   b. thrust   c. quip

8. pull : drag :: push : _____
   a. thrust   b. bestow   c. quip

9. disorder : rebellion :: order : _____
   a. convention   b. stimulus   c. intensity

10. enemy : forgive :: mentor : _____
    a. thrust   b. acknowledge   c. quip

UNIT 4 Vocabulary in Math, Science, and Technology

Vocabulary and Mathematics

Get Ready to Read About Mathematics

Most college degrees require at least a semester of mathematics such as college algebra, pre-calculus, calculus, or statistics because these courses are prerequisites for many majors. Occasionally, students complain that one of the most challenging aspects of math is trying to find solutions to word problems. Sometimes, what hinders their ability to find a solution is not the process, but the vocabulary. In this selection from a college algebra textbook, you will read about some real-life applications. Before you read, however, consider the following word parts. The meanings of some have been provided. Recall what you learned in Chapter 1 and fill in the blanks for the others.

1. The prefix *in-* means _____.

2. The root *equ* means _____.

3. The root *fin-* means _____.

4. The suffix *-able* means *able to* and usually indicates an _____.

5. The suffix *-fy* means *cause to become* and indicates a _____.

| constant | factor | infinite | pi | signify |
| equation | formula | meter | radius | variable |

FORMULAS

Many applications of mathematics involve relationships among two or more quantities. An **equation** that represents such a relationship will use two or more letters and is known as a formula. Although most of the letters in this book represent **variables,** some—like c in $E = mc^2$ or π in $C = \pi d$ – represent **constants.** (The symbol *pi* π **signifies** the **infinite** decimal that begins 3.14159.)

Evaluating Formulas

Example 1

Outdoor concerts. The formula $d = 344t$ can be used to determine how far d, in **meters,** sound travels through room-temperature air in one second. In 2003, the Dave Matthews Band performed in New York City's Central Park. Fans near the back of the crowd experienced a 0.9-sec time lag between the time each word was pronounced on stage (as shown on large video monitors) and the time the sound reached their ears. How far were these fans from the stage?

Solution We substitute 0.9 for t in $d = 344t$ and calculate d:

$$d = 344(0.9) = 309.6$$

The fans were about 309.6 m from the stage.

Example 2

Circumference of a circle. The formula $C = 2\pi r$ gives the circumference C of a circle with **radius** r. Solve for r.

Solution: The circumference is the distance around the circle.

Given a radius r, we can use this equation to find a circle's circumference C.	$C = 2\pi r$ $\dfrac{C}{2\pi} = \dfrac{2\pi r}{2\pi}$	We want this letter alone. Dividing both sides by 2π
Given a circle's circumference C, we can use this equation to find the radius r.	$\dfrac{C}{2\pi} = r$	

To Solve a Formula for a Given Letter

1. If the letter for which you are solving appears in a fraction, use the multiplication principle to clear fractions.
2. Isolate the term(s), with the letter you are solving for on one side of the equation.
3. If two or more terms contain the letter you are solving for, **factor** the letter out.
4. Multiply or divide to solve for the letter in question.

—Adapted from *Elementary & Intermediate Algebra* by Bittinger et al., pp. 97-99.
© 2006, 2002 Pearson Education, Inc. Reprinted by permission of Pearson Education, Inc. All rights reserved.

VISUAL VOCABULARY

To convert the distance of this

train route from miles to _____, you would multiply the number of miles by 1609.3.

   a. equations
   b. meters

Courtesy of Microsoft.

EXERCISE **1** Context Clues

Refer to the previous passage and use context clues from the sentences below to determine the definition of each of the following words in **bold** print. Do not consult a dictionary.

1. constant (kŏn´stənt) n.

When Ben calculated his monthly budget, he knew the one **constant,** the number that would not change each month, was the amount he would spend on rent; everything else seemed to increase consistently each month.

_____ **Constant** means

a. changing number.

b. negative number.

c. fixed number; steady feature.

d. unknown number.

2. equation (ĭ-kwā´zhən) n.

During World War II, an engineer worked the **equation** to build a bridge that would lower several meters to allow large ships to pass.

_____ **Equation** means

a. unchanging number.

b. series.

c. number sentence that equals a solution.

d. fixed point that equals a product.

3. factor (făk´tər) v.

As the student engineers in the rental truck listened to the grating of metal against stone, they realized they had forgotten to **factor** in the height of the truck against the low clearance of the old underpass on the campus.

_____ **Factor** means

a. divide.

b. add.

c. subtract to determine the difference.

d. figure in to determine the product.

4. formula (fôr´myə-lə) n.

A new line of FlexFuel cars will be able to run on either gasoline or E85 Ethanol that has a **formula** of 85% ethanol and 15% gasoline.

_____ **Formula** means

a. relationship of numbers or letters.

b. number sentence without a verb.

c. successful project.

d. numerical evaluation.

5. infinite (ĭn′fə-nĭt) adj.
The fact that some numbers are **infinite** and unending is indicated by the Greek symbol ∞.

_____ **Infinite** means
   a. limitless.
   b. medium time frame of existence.
   c. sum of three numbers that equal more than zero.
   d. any sum of more than three numbers.

6. meter (mē′tər) n.
A football field is measured in yards, but in **meters** it would be about 91.44.

_____ **Meter** means
   a. any sum.
   b. difference of yards and feet.
   c. measurement of 39.37 inches.
   d. measurement no longer in use.

7. pi (pī) n.
The magic number **pi** is considered very versatile because it appears in a variety of places.

_____ **Pi** means
   a. product of 3.14 and 10.
   b. all sums over 3.14.
   c. any variable.
   d. constant of 3.14.

8. radius (rā′dē-əs) n.
When Danny changed his tires from 215 to 235, which have a **radius** of 37.02 inches, he also raised the height of the truck by 4 inches.

_____ **Radius** means
   a. length of a line from one side of circle to the other.
   b. straight line extended from the center of a circle or sphere.
   c. distance around a circle.
   d. degrees of a right angle.

9. signify (sĭg′nə-fī′) v.
Greek symbols such as Σ and ∂ **signify** specific math functions.

_____ **Signify** means
   a. transfer.
   b. end.
   c. indicate.
   d. promote.

10. variable (vâr′ē-ə-bəl) n.

   The equation $d = rt$ contains three **variables** representing the sentence: Distance will equal the rate of speed multiplied by the time.

   _____ **Variable** means
   - a. predictor.
   - b. organization.
   - c. expectation.
   - d. that which has no fixed amount or number; anything changeable.

EXERCISE 2 Word Sorts

Synonyms

Match the word to the synonyms or definitions that follow each blank.

1. _____ international measurement of 39.7 inches

2. _____ transcendental number of 3.14159; 16th letter of the Greek alphabet

3. _____ blueprint; code; specifications; equation

4. _____ method; canon; credo; formula

5. _____ range; expanse; semi-diameter; ambit

Antonyms

Select the letter of the word(s) with the opposite meaning.

_____ 6. factor
   - a. figure in
   - b. ignore
   - c. consider
   - d. determine

_____ 7. constant
   - a. fixed value
   - b. unchanging value
   - c. variable
   - d. set amount

_____ 8. infinite
   - a. unlimited
   - b. defiant
   - c. definite
   - d. limited

_____ 9. variable
   - a. constant
   - b. changing value
   - c. surprise
   - d. instability

_____ 10. signify
   - a. designate
   - b. keep secret
   - c. appoint
   - d. acknowledge

EXERCISE 3 Fill in the Blank

Use context clues to determine the word that best completes each sentence.

1. "The one _____ in our lives," remarked the wife of a military officer, "is our sense of family, and no matter where we travel, we know we have our own close community at home."

2. After the politicians _____ in the increase in the cost of living, which included a sudden jump in the price of gasoline, they realized that a 5% wage increase would still not be enough for state employees.

3. The investigators began their search for clues along a 500-foot _____ in all directions from the crime scene.

4. When he learned that one of his football players was skipping classes, the coach suspended the player from the team because he knew that missing college classes was one part of the _____ for failure.

5. As astrophysicists discovered that the universe is expanding, they began to theorize that outer space is _____.

6. The book, *The Life of Pi,* is not about the mathematical symbol _____; it is about a young Indian with that nickname who is adrift at sea in the same boat with a hungry Bengal tiger.

7. When the American flag is flown upside down, it _____ that someone is in distress and emergency personnel should be alerted.

8. Lindsay stared at the algebra problem, trying to remember how to solve the _____, $x^2 - 5 = 4x$.

9. When planning a vacation, the engineer agreed to consider the possibility of some _____ out of his control such as weather, long lines, and heavy traffic.

10. As a swimmer for the University of Tennessee, Josh swam 8,000 _____ each day, and then one week before a meet he tapered his practice to 2,000 meters a day.

EXERCISE 4 Application

Using context clues, insert the vocabulary word in the appropriate blank. A part-of-speech clue is given for each vocabulary word.

"I have lived a full, rich life without mathematics," groaned Kim, "and I do not see the need to take a class in it now when I am a theater major!"

Dr. Yost smiled because she had heard other advisees make the same complaint when they realized they had failed to **(1)** (v.) _____ in a math class, which was a requirement for graduation. What frightens students is the idea of taking a course in which their background knowledge is minimal—developed from courses taken years earlier. For example, many college students took high school algebra in the 9th grade. That is when they learned that in the **(2)** (n.) _____: $6x - 7 = 2x + 5$, they were to solve for the **(3)** (n.) _____ x. The concept of **(4)** (n.) _____—that fixed number in mathematics—likewise was something they had not considered for four or five years. This did not **(5)** (v.) _____ a lack of intelligence—only a lack of practice.

Those years of memorizing **(6)** (n.) _____ such as $y = \cos x$ were in the past, or so they thought. Although the despair seemed heavy in the room, Dr. Yost began to explain the reality of mathematics in their everyday lives.

To some she explained that calculating the distance for a **(7)** (n.) _____ could be helpful in engineering or physical education or even in their study abroad adventures where the metric system is used. And using **(8)** (n.) _____, she explained, to discover the **(9)** (n.) _____ of a circle is important in a variety of careers from urban planning to criminal justice.

"Math, you see, is actually a necessary constant in our lives—something we can always count on being there," said Dr. Yost. "We use it to solve problems, to stretch our logic, to create order in our world. Numbers do not lie. In fact, there is something very beautiful in numbers. Actually, mathematics is art."

Then with a mischievous twinkle in her eye, she added, "And if you study well, you can even learn an **(10)** (adj.) _____ number of ways of how to lie with numbers."

Stop and Think

 Read the following word problem from a business application. Then fill in the blanks with the appropriate math terms used to determine the solution.

Problem. Hours worked. A carpenter charges $25 an hour. How many hours did she work if she billed the bank a total of $53,400 for three different jobs for new trim work, book cases, and a reception area?

—Adapted from *Elementary & Intermediate Algebra* by Bittinger et al., p. 10. © 2006, 2002 Pearson Education, Inc. Reprinted by permission of Pearson Education, Inc. All rights reserved.

Know	Need to Know	Don't Need to Know	How to Calculate
Charges $25/hour	How many hours worked?	Three different jobs	Division
Billed $53,400			

In this problem, the _____ is $25.00 an hour because that number does not change. To solve the _____, the student must divide the total cost of the jobs by the fee per hour. The solution is _____ hours worked.

 Go to **www.joyofpi.com** and list some details about pi on your own paper.

14

Vocabulary and Geology

Get Ready to Read About Geology

Geology is the study of the earth's origin, history, and structure. Since many college programs require a lab science, geology is a course you may choose to study. Before you read the selection on the types of volcanic eruptions, consider what you already know about the following word parts. The meanings of some have been provided. Recall what you learned in Chapter 1 and fill in the blanks for the others.

1. The prefix *dis-* means *apart, away, in different directions*.

2. The root *lum* means *light*.

3. The suffix *-ive* means *of, like, related to*, or *being* and indicates an

   _____.

4. The suffix *-ous* means *related to* and indicates an _____.

| arc | distinctive | incandescent | luminous | rivulet |
| avalanche | flank | laden | molten | summit |

TYPES OF VOLCANIC ERUPTIONS

During an episode of activity, a volcano commonly displays a **distinctive** pattern or type of behavior. One type of eruption is a Vesuvian eruption; during this type of eruption, great quantities of ash-**laden** gas are violently discharged. These gases form a cauliflower-shaped cloud high above the volcano. A second kind of eruption is the Strombolian. In a Strombolian-type eruption, huge clots of **molten** lava burst from the **summit** crater to form **luminous arcs** through the sky. The lava collects on the **flanks** of the cone, and then lava clots combine to stream down the slopes in fiery **rivulets.** Another kind of eruption is the Vulcanian type. In this eruption, a dense cloud of ash-laden gas explodes from the crater and rises high above the peak. Steaming ash forms a whitish cloud near the upper level of the cone. A fourth kind of eruption is a Peléan or Nuée Ardente (glowing cloud) eruption. A large amount of gas, dust, ash, and **incandescent** lava fragments are blown out of a central crater, fall back, and form tongue-like glowing **avalanches.** These avalanches move down slopes at speeds as great as 100 miles per hour.

—From D. J. Henry, *The Effective Reader,* Updated Edition. Pearson Longman, 2004.
Reprinted by permission of Pearson Education, Inc., Glenview, IL. Adapted from U.S.
Geological Survey, "Types of Volcanic Eruptions."

VISUAL VOCABULARY

These bluebonnets of Texas are

_____ flowers of the state.

a. distinctive
b. incandescent

Courtesy of Gabrielle Fletcher.

EXERCISE 1 Context Clues

Refer to the previous passage and use context clues from the sentences below to determine the definition of each of the following words in **bold** print. Do not consult a dictionary.

1. arc (ärk) n.
During the thunderstorm, we noticed **arcs** of light coming from a nearby transformer just before the power went out.

_____ **Arc** means

a. stone.

b. angle

c. curve.

d. line.

2. avalanche (ăv′ə-lănch′) n

When the ski patrol feared a possible **avalanche,** they closed the trails until conditions were safe again.

_____ **Avalanche** means

a. hurricane.

b. earthquake.

c. rapid moving thunderstorm.

d. large moving mass of snow, ice, and rock.

3. distinctive (dĭ-stĭngk′tĭv) adj.

The two candidates for mayor were so different: one spoke in a **distinctive** and clear voice, while the other mumbled uncomfortably throughout the debate.

_____ **Distinctive** means

a. unique.

b. typical.

c. famous.

d. light.

4. flank (flăngk) n.

The soldiers in the left **flank** were ordered to remain in position until those in the lead could determine if the area was safe.

_____ **Flank** means

a. middle.

b. lead.

c. end.

d. side.

5. incandescent (ĭn′kən-dĕs′ənt) adj.

Thomas Edison is credited with creating the **incandescent** light bulb—an invention that has changed people's lives.

_____ **Incandescent** means

a. dark.

b. glowing with heat.

c. sensitive.

d. dull.

6. laden (lād′n) adj.

The wedding cake was **laden** with ribbons of icing and fresh flowers.

_____ **Laden** means

a. loaded.

b. corrected.

c. shareed.

d. dug.

7. luminous (lo͞o′mə-nəs) adj.
   The **luminous** full moon glowed against a tent of stars, casting a dazzling shine on the frozen snow on the distant pasture.

   _____ **Luminous** means

   a. falling.   c. bright; clear.
   b. frightening.   d. common; ordinary.

8. molten (mōl′tən) adj.
   Demonstrating his art, the glassblower twisted the pipe slowly and said, "**Molten** glass is like honey on a hot day."

   _____ **Molten** means

   a. ordinary.   c. stiff.
   b. sweet.   d. melted.

9. rivulet (rĭv′yə-lĭt) n.
   After hiking for hours, we wiped **rivulets** of sweat from our faces, eager for cooler temperatures after sunset.

   _____ **Rivulet** means

   a. small stream.   c. light flash.
   b. cushion.   d. dryness.

10. summit (sŭm′ĭt) n.
    Jan Krakauer's book *Into Thin Air* recounts his quest to reach the **summit** of Mt. Everest and the tragedies that fell upon his expedition.

    _____ **Summit** means

    a. foundation.   c. cave.
    b. peak.   d. base.

EXERCISE 2 Word Sorts

Synonyms

Match the word to the synonyms or definitions that follow each blank.

1. _____ glowing; radiant; shining; gleaming

2. _____ small stream; runnel; trickle; rill

3. _____ a mass of fast moving snow; ice; and rock

4. _____ weighted; heavy; fraught; loaded

5. _____ curve; bow; hook; tracery

Antonyms

Select the letter of the word(s) with the opposite meaning.

_____ **6.** luminous
   a. happy   b. heavy   c. light   d. dull

_____ **7.** flank
   a. end   b. side   c. arch   d. curve

_____ **8.** molten
   a. soft   b. crunchy   c. solid   d. liquefied

_____ **9.** summit
   a. top   b. base   c. height   d. length

_____ **10.** distinctive
   a. extraordinary   b. ordinary   c. valuable   d. honest

EXERCISE **3** Fill in the Blank

Use context clues to determine the word that best completes each sentence.

1. My grandparents' garden, which is _____ with vegetables, is the result of constant and careful attention.

2. Recently, an earthquake caused a sudden _____ that ploughed down the mountain and stopped just short of the old ski resort.

3. While in Hawaii, we trekked near a live volcano that was spewing hot, _____ lava.

4. This spring, the pollen count has been so high that we are finding yellow _____ along our sidewalks and driveways.

5. For the queen's 80th birthday, crowds gathered to enjoy the _____ of light as fireworks illuminated the night sky.

6. One of Ben's classmates has a _____ tattoo of a bridge emblazoned on the back of his neck.

7. Both trails along the _____ of Mary's Rock lead to the same point at the top.

8. Fluorescent light bulbs usually last longer than _____ ones.

9. At the _____ of the mountain, we enjoyed a panoramic view of four states.

10. As evening approached at the Shakespeare festival, actors sold
_____ jewelry that glowed radiantly in the night.

EXERCISE ☑ **4** Application

Using context clues, insert the vocabulary word in the appropriate blank. A
part-of-speech clue is given for each vocabulary word.

In Roman mythology, Vulcan was the son of Jupiter and Juno. His
counterpart in Greek mythology was Hephaestus. According to Roman
myths, Vulcan was the god of fire and volcanoes as well as the maker of
art, iron, arms, and armor. He was also the Romans' explanation for
the existence of volcanoes and the **(1)** (n.) _____ of fire-
filled light and **(2)** (n.) _____ of lava that flowed in
(3) (n.) _____ to nearby towns. Thus, it was believed that
Vulcan's smithy was located beneath Mount Etna, an active volcano on the
east coast of Sicily. Because of the violent impact of the eruptions, the impressive **(4)** (adj.) _____ light show needed explanation. And
so the myth of Vulcan was born.

With a **(5)** (n.) _____ of 10, 991 feet, Mt. Etna remains the
largest volcano in Europe. Also, because several eruptions over the years have
caused **(6)** (adj.) _____ lava to travel down the slopes, it is 71
feet lower than it was in 1865. It remains one of the most
(7) (adj.) _____ natural landmarks in Italy.

The myth of Vulcan also prompted a yearly festival each August 23rd.
During the festival of Vulcanalia, small fish and animals were thrown into a
fire as part of a ritual to honor the god. Vulcan's shrine in the Forum
Romanum was called *Volcanal* and it played an important role in civic rituals
of the Roman Kingdom.

According to mythology, Jupiter found it necessary to punish mankind for stealing the secrets of fire. Thus, he ordered the other gods to make Pandora a poisoned gift for man. Vulcan's contribution to the beautiful and foolish Pandora was to mold her from clay and to give her form. He also made the thrones for the other gods on Mount Olympus.

Today, volcanoes still remain a threat. In May 2006, Mount Merapi began to glow with the **(8)** (adj.) _____ molten lava on the **(9)** (n.) _____ of its summit, sending a warning to the inhabitants of Jukarta, Indonesia. Once again, humans were humbly reminded of the power with which mountains are **(10)** (v.) _____ deep inside—something no ritual can really prevent.

—Adapted from http://en.wikipedia.org/wiki/Vulcan
(retrieved 5/12/06)

Stop and Think

 Using a vocabulary word from this chapter, write a caption for this painting by Diego Velasquez depicting the forge of Vulcan.

_____

_____

_____

_____

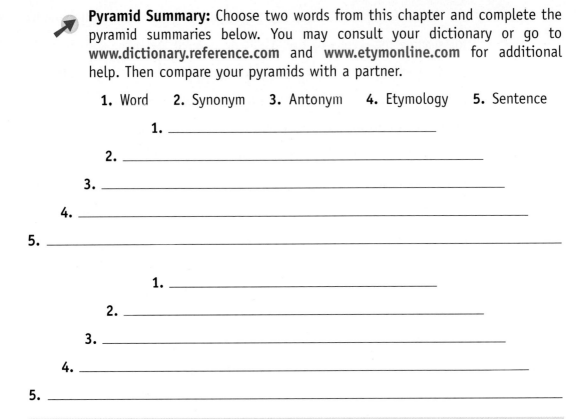

Pyramid Summary: Choose two words from this chapter and complete the pyramid summaries below. You may consult your dictionary or go to **www.dictionary.reference.com** and **www.etymonline.com** for additional help. Then compare your pyramids with a partner.

1. Word   **2.** Synonym   **3.** Antonym   **4.** Etymology   **5.** Sentence

1. _____

2. _____

3. _____

4. _____

5. _____

1. _____

2. _____

3. _____

4. _____

5. _____

CHAPTER 15

Vocabulary and Biology

Get Ready to Read About Biology

Many college students choose to take biology to fulfill the lab science requirement for their curriculum because they have prior knowledge of the subject if they took high school biology. Also, many nursing programs now require Biology 101 as a prerequisite for their course in Anatomy and Physiology. This selection on biodiversity is from a chapter on the environment in a college biology textbook. Before you read the selection, predict what you think the word *diversity*, which means *differences*, has to do with biology and the environment. Next, consider what you already know about the following word parts. The meanings of some have been provided. Recall what you learned in Chapter 1 and fill in the blanks for the others.

1. The prefix *com-* means *with, together*.

2. The prefix *con-* means _____.

3. The prefix *de-* means _____.

4. The root *bio* means _____.

5. The root *eco* means *house, dwelling*.

6. The suffix *-ate* means *cause to become* or *make* and usually indicates a

   _____.

7. The suffix *-ive* means _____ and usually indicates an

   _____ .

8. The suffix *-ous* means _____ and usually indicates an

   _____ .

---

biosphere	contiguous	demise	dwindle	moderate
component	cumulative	derivative	ecosystem	secrete

THE THREE LEVELS OF BIODIVERSITY

Biodiversity, short for biological diversity, has three main **components.** The first is diversity of ecosystems. Each ecosystem, be it a rain forest, desert, or coral reef, has a unique biological community and characteristic patterns of energy flow and chemical cycling. And each **ecosystem** has a unique impact on the entire **biosphere.** For example, the productive "pastures" of phytoplankton in the oceans help **moderate** the greenhouse effect by consuming massive quantities of atmospheric CO_2 for photosynthesis and shell building (many microscopic protists in plankton **secrete** shells of bicarbonate, a **derivative** of CO_2). Some ecosystems are being erased from the biosphere at an astonishing rate. For example, the **cumulative** area of all tropical rain forests is only about the size of the 48 **contiguous** United States, and we lose an area equal to the state of West Virginia each year.

The second **component** of biodiversity is the variety of species that make up the biological community of any ecosystem. And the third component is the genetic variation within each species. As you have learned previously, the loss of genetic diversity—by severe reduction in population size, for example—can hasten the **demise** of a **dwindling** species.

Though human impact reaches all three levels of biodiversity, most of the research focus so far has been on species extinction.

—Adapted from *Essential Biology,* 2nd Edition, by Neil A. Campbell, Jane B. Reece, and Eric J. Simon. San Francisco: Pearson Benjamin Cummings, 2004, p. 452. Reprinted by permission of Pearson Education, Inc., Glenview, IL.

VISUAL VOCABULARY

These biodomes in Cornwall, England, are part of the Eden project, which contains the only

_____ of a manmade rain forest in the world.

  a. ecosystem
  b. demise

Susan Kunchandy

EXERCISE 1 Context Clues

Refer to the previous passage and use context clues from the sentences below to determine the definition of each of the following words in **bold** print. Do not consult a dictionary.

1. biosphere (bī′ə-sfîr′) n.
   Experiments to create a manmade **biosphere** require a dome-like structure enveloping an area that can sustain living organisms.

   _____ **Biosphere** means
        a. area around the Arctic.   c. atmosphere.
        b. outer space.   d. part of the world in which life exists.

2. component (kəm-pō′nənt) n.
   An important **component** of the new veterinary program on campus is the ethics course that deals with moral decisions in the treatment of animals.

   _____ **Component** means
        a. test.   c. portion.
        b. plan.   d. frame.

3. contiguous (kən-tĭg′yoo-əs) adj.
Although the grand prize in the magazine contest was an all-expense-paid trip to anywhere in the **contiguous** United States, we did not enter because we wanted to visit Hawaii instead.

_____ **Contiguous** means
    a. fighting area.   c. competitive.
    b. touching a boundary.   d. stable.

4. cumulative (kyoom′yə-lā′tĭv) adj.
After a difficult first semester, Ian had to work twice as hard to raise his grade point average since he knew that he would need a **cumulative** GPA of 2.0 to graduate.

_____ **Cumulative** means
    a. current.   c. overall.
    b. single.   d. first.

5. demise (dĭ-mīz′) n.
"I started hyperventilating and imagining my own **demise**," exclaimed Kim, "when I read the passage about the process of drowning in Sebastian Junger's _The Perfect Storm_."

_____ **Demise** means
    a. death.   c. isolation.
    b. success.   d. loneliness.

6. derivative (dĭ-rĭv′ə-tĭv) n.
By studying the **derivative** of a word (that is, learning its roots, prefixes, and suffixes), we can better remember its definition.

_____ **Derivative** means
    a. origin.   c. sensitivity.
    b. work.   d. sensibility.

7. dwindle (dwĭn′dl) v.
Our enthusiasm for our philosophy class began to **dwindle** little by little each week as we realized how difficult the course actually was.

_____ **Dwindle** means
    a. remain unchanged.   c. increase rapidly.
    b. drop suddenly.   d. decrease slowly.

8. ecosystem (ē′kō-sĭs′təm) n.
Fertilizers contaminate the groundwater, which can then negatively affect the **ecosystems** of the marine life in the bay.

_____ **Ecosystem** means
- a. complex of organisms functioning as a unit.
- b. mammals and their parasites.
- c. plants.
- d. known atmosphere.

9. moderate (mŏd′ər-′āt) v.
Good negotiation skills require that you learn to **moderate** the level of angry expression so parties can communicate rather than compete.

_____ **Moderate** means
- a. increase.
- b. lessen.
- c. involve.
- d. stir up.

10. secrete (sĭ-krēt′) v.
When a mosquito bites, it **secretes** a substance that causes an allergic reaction in your skin, which then creates the itching sensation.

_____ **Secrete** means
- a. absorb.
- b. produce.
- c. bite.
- d. surround.

EXERCISE 2 Word Sorts

Synonyms

Match the word to the synonyms or definitions that follow each blank.

1. _____ complex where organisms live as a unit

2. _____ root; origin; out-growth; spin-off

3. _____ portion of the earth where living organisms thrive

4. _____ death; failure; end; departure

5. _____ decelerate; taper; delay; slow down

Antonyms

Select the letter of the word(s) with the opposite meaning.

_____ **6.** secrete
   a. absorb   b. place   c. instill   d. deposit

_____ **7.** contiguous

    a. separate   b. touching   c. large   d. famous

_____ **8.** component

    a. part   b. fairness   c. interest   d. whole

_____ **9.** cumulative

    a. adding   b. subtracting   c. multiplying   d. reasoning

_____ **10.** dwindle

    a. trickle   b. increase   c. taper   d. decrease slowly

EXERCISE 3 Fill in the Blank

Use context clues to determine the word that best completes each sentence.

1. As the gas supply _____ a little each week, the public began to grow more concerned, and people began to spend more time at home and less time on the road.

2. Following the _____ of his aunt and uncle, Peter Parker began his quest to fight evil forces as Spider Man.

3. Ethanol, a _____ of corn, has been added to refined gasoline to decrease petroleum consumption and reduce pollution.

4. States _____ to Texas include New Mexico, Oklahoma, Arkansas, and Louisiana.

5. One technique to get a child's attention is to calmly _____ your voice rather than raise it in anger or frustration.

6. The _____ effect of excessive stress hormones can lead to clogged arteries.

7. The _____ of an entertainment center might include a DVD player, CD changer, TV, amplifiers, and surround-sound speakers.

8. Beeswax is _____ by honey bees and is used in making candles, polish, jewelry molds, casings for cheese, and even filling the holes in the assembly of pool tables.

9. Geochemists (that is, scientists who study the chemistry of the earth) see the _____ as but one of four separate components of the geochemical make-up of the earth rather than the only area where all living organisms on Earth exist.

10. Environmentalists are watchful over every _____—whether it is a desert or lakes or marsh or forest or tide pool—because protecting units of living organisms ultimately preserves the balance of the Earth.

EXERCISE ☐4 Application

Using context clues, insert the vocabulary word in the appropriate blank. A part-of-speech clue is given for each vocabulary word.

As of the mid-1990s, more than 50% of Americans live in cities. Those who live in a rural, or country, setting now make up a small **(1)** (n.) _____ of the nation's population. For many, learning about an **(2)** (n.) _____ of a forest or marsh or seashore is something they only read about, but never experience firsthand. As a result, many parts of the **(3)** (n.) _____, the area on earth where life thrives, are not a personal matter, so the **(4)** (n.) _____ of endangered species of plants and animals such as the polar bears of the Arctic or the periwinkle flower of the rain forest do not seem so critical. Yet, those who are aware of a cancer drug that is a **(5)** (n.) _____ of that periwinkle recognize how interconnected humans are with nature.

Likewise, the **(6)** (adj.) _____ effect of people crowding in cities presents new problems. Just learning to **(7)** (v.) _____ the noise level in a tightly packed community with **(8)** (adj.) _____ homes, such as row houses or condominiums next to each other, can also cause human compassion to **(9)** (v.) _____ and frustration to rise.

One of the reasons students study biology in college is for awareness—not just about the details such as how a spider can **(10)** (v.) _____ its venom in its prey or even how diverse rain forests have become. Instead, the course also encourages students to become good stewards of the earth and caregivers to its inhabitants, thus encouraging a productive and protected life for all.

Stop and Think

 Fill in the blanks with other forms of the word, and then include the definition of each.

Noun	Verb	Adjective
_____	_____	cumulative
derivative	_____	
_____	moderate	_____
_____	secrete	

 Go to **http://en.wikipedia.org/wiki/Biosphere_2** and read about Biosphere 2, and in the space below, fill in the following information.

Who or What is this about? _____

What is its purpose? _____

Where is it located? _____

When was it constructed? _____

Why was it built? _____

How was it built? _____

16 Vocabulary and the Internet

Get Ready to Read About the Internet

Most college students are computer savvy and have been using the Internet for communication, research, and online shopping. However, learning computer terminology as well as the background of the Internet can help students be more informed about a rapidly changing tool that has had a major impact on nearly everyone's life. Before you read the selection, however, consider what you already know about the following word parts.

1. The prefix *con-* means _____.

2. The prefix *infra-* means _____.

3. The prefix *pro-* means _____.

4. The prefix *syn-* means _____.

5. The prefix *tele-* means _____.

6. The root *phon* means _____.

7. The root *poli-* means _____.

8. The suffix *-ous* means _____ and usually indicates an

    _____.

9. The suffix *-tion* means *action, state* and usually indicates a

    _____.

| bandwidth | congestion | infrastructure | metropolitan | synchronous |
| circuitous | data | latency | mobility | telephony |

LIMITATIONS OF INTERNET I

Much of the Internet's current **infrastructure** is several decades old (equivalent to a century in Internet time). It suffers from a number of limitations, including:

- *Bandwidth limitations.* There is insufficient capacity throughout the backbone, the **metropolitan** switching centers, and most importantly, the "last mile" to the house and small business. The result is slow service (**congestion**) and a very limited ability to handle video and voice traffic.
- *Quality of service limitations.* Today's information packets take a **circuitous** route to get to their final destinations. This creates the phenomenon of **latency**—delays in messages caused by the uneven flow of information packets through the network. In the case of e-mail, latency is not noticeable. However, with streaming video and **synchronous** communication, such as a telephone call, latency is noticeable to the user and perceived as "jerkiness" in movies or delays in voice communication. Today's Internet uses "best efforts" quality of service (QOS), which makes no guarantees about when or whether **data** will be delivered, and provides each packet with the same level of service, no matter who the user is or what type of data is contained in the packet. A higher level of service quality is required if the Internet is to keep expanding into new services (such as video on demand or **telephony**).
- *Network architecture limitations.* Today, a thousand requests for a single music track from a central server will result in a thousand efforts by the server to download the music to each requesting client. This slows down network performance as the same music track is sent out a thousand times to clients that might be located in the same metropolitan area. This is very different from television, where the program is broadcast once to millions of homes.
- *Language development limitations.* HTML, the language of Web pages, is fine for text and simple graphics, but poor at defining and communicating "rich documents" such as databases, business documents, or graphics. The tags used to define an HTML page are fixed and generic.
- *Wired Internet.* The Internet is based on cables—fiber-optic and coaxial copper cables. Copper cables use a centuries-old technology, and fiber-optic cable is expensive to place underground. The wired nature of the Internet restricts **mobility** of users.

Now imagine an Internet at least 100 times as powerful as today's Internet, one that is not subjected to the limitations of bandwidth, protocols, architecture, physical connections, and language detailed above. Welcome to the world of Internet II.

—Adapted from Laudon/Traver, *E-commerce: Business, Technology, Society,* pp. 147-148.
© 2004 Kenneth Laudon & Carol Traver. Reproduced by permission of Pearson Education, Inc. All rights reserved.

VISUAL VOCABULARY

A computer on a college campus often has more _____, so the connection is much faster than a home computer would have.

a. bandwidth
b. congestion

Susan Pongratz

EXERCISE **1** Context Clues

Refer to the previous passage and use context clues from the sentences below to determine the definition of each of the following words in **bold** print. Do not consult a dictionary.

1. bandwidth (bănd-wĭdth) n.
Until we switched to a digital signal line with greater **bandwidth,** our Internet connection was so slow it seemed to be moving through a clogged pixie stick.

_____ **Bandwidth** means
a. capacity for data transfer.   c. length of a parade.
b. length of computer cable.   d. width of a band of people.

2. circuitous (sər-kyōō′ĭ-təs) adj.
   The directions from the rental car agency led us through a winding and **circuitous** route on narrow roads because of several construction areas on the main highways.

   _____ **Circuitous** means
   - a. simple.
   - b. slender.
   - c. twisty.
   - d. straight.

3. congestion (kən-jĕs′chən) n.
   After the news broke about the celebrity's surprise marriage, visits to his website caused so much **congestion** that it had to be shut down for several days.

   _____ **Congestion** means
   - a. bottleneck.
   - b. break.
   - c. opening.
   - d. clearing.

4. data (dā′tə) n.
   After collecting the **data** from the survey, we met to interpret the results and then adjust our marketing strategies as a result.

   _____ **Data** means
   - a. surprise.
   - b. factual information.
   - c. guesswork.
   - d. fictional information.

5. infrastructure (ĭn′frə-strŭk′chər) n.
   Although the city seemed fine after the earthquake, reports began to arrive indicating that the **infrastructure** was damaged, including the water lines, electrical lines, and communication connections.

   _____ **Infrastructure** means
   - a. formlessness.
   - b. network of support.
   - c. measure of success.
   - d. global view.

6. latency (lāt′n-sē) n.
   Although we had video and audio connection with our father on the aircraft carrier in the Mediterranean halfway across the world, our conversation was punctuated by gaps because of **latency** and the interrupted time for transmission.

   _____ **Latency** means
   - a. rapid connection.
   - b. quick arrangement.
   - c. silence.
   - d. delay.

7. metropolitan (mĕt′rə-pŏl′ĭ-tən) adj.
   Jennifer wanted to work in a large **metropolitan** museum in a city such as New York or Boston, while her roommate Anna preferred to look for a job in a small rural town.

   _____ **Metropolitan** means
   a. country.
   b. far-reaching.
   c. relating to the city, sometimes including suburbs.
   d. relating to the country.

8. mobility (mō-bĭl′ĭ-tē) n.
   As communities spread beyond the cities, traffic increases if public transportation is not presented as a reliable means of **mobility**.

   _____ **Mobility** means
   a. revolution.
   b. misrule.
   c. movement.
   d. disobedience.

9. synchronous (sĭng′krə-nəs) adj.
   In **synchronous** communication that takes place in a chat room, messages are sent and received instantly, whereas in asynchronous communication such as e-mail or discussion boards, the replies may not be sent for several days.

   _____ **Synchronous** means
   a. happening at the same time. c. moving in opposite directions.
   b. happening at different times. d. having the same sound.

10. telephony (tə-lĕf′ə-nē) n.
    Although cell phones are becoming more popular, so is the **telephony** feature on computers to process voices over distance, so Internet business meetings can be held.

    _____ **Telephony** means
    a. mental processes.
    b. voice communication.
    c. mind reading.
    d. text messaging.

EXERCISE **2** Word Sorts

Synonyms

Match the word to the synonyms or definitions that follow each blank.

1. _____ framework; underlying structure; basic foundation; underlying system

2. _____ measurement of the amount of transferable data

3. _____ moving; progression; motion; advancement

4. _____ delay in computer transmission

5. _____ information; documents; details; facts

Antonyms

Select the letter of the word(s) with the opposite meaning.

_____ 6. synchronous
    a. accidental   b. simultaneous   c. concurrent   d. timely

_____ 7. circuitous
    a. labyrinthine   b. indirect   c. winding   d. direct

_____ 8. metropolitan
    a. global   b. urban   c. rural   d. popular

_____ 9. congestion
    a. jam   b. emptiness   c. bottleneck   d. blockage

_____ 10. telephony
    a. silence   b. voice communication   c. imaging
    d. movement

EXERCISE 3 Fill in the Blank

Use context clues to determine the word that best completes each sentence.

1. Shopping online is similar to mall shopping since both have a great deal of

   _____ around holiday seasons, with slow response time and crowded stores.

2. Millenials, current college students, are used to multi-tasking, and are comfortable doing Internet research, writing e-mail messages, and

   sending several _____ Instant Message communications in one sitting.

3. Writer Barbara Kingsolver grew up in a small rural area of Kentucky and believes her appreciation for nature developed in the woods behind her house—something she would have missed in the big city atmosphere of a

   more _____ area.

4. The _____, or channel capacity, of a computer describes the amount and speed of data that can be processed, and is measured in MB/s, or megabytes per second.

5. Wireless networking in Central Park in New York City is a free service that provides _____ for anyone who wants to work on a laptop outside and be able to move around.

6. Whereas software engineering tools refer to the _____ of computing, in urban planning the term can also refer to highways, public utilities, and public services.

7. Whether it involves communications, operations, or mechanics, _____ refers to the time delay from the beginning of a project until the first effect is felt.

8. Advances in computer technology now make _____ for voice communication possible, and some analysts predict that taste and smell will be the next senses available over the Internet.

9. Numbers, words, and images that are accepted as "givens" are all examples of _____ that can be used to support a claim or statement of belief.

10. Although many people think Abraham Lincoln followed a straight path to the White House as the 16th President of the United States, a quick look at his life reveals a more _____ route as poor farmer of illiterate parents, surveyor, state representative, militia captain, failed businessman, self-educated prairie lawyer, and finally president.

EXERCISE 4 Application

Using context clues, insert the vocabulary word in the appropriate blank. A part-of-speech clue is given for each vocabulary word.

Education is often the key to a new career, so Norm decided to register for classes at a community college. Because he did not live in a **(1)** (adj.) _____ area, however, a distance learning course provided a way for him to earn a college degree despite his isolation in the country. When

Norm decided to take the online class, he discovered he needed more than a computer to succeed. Appropriate **(2)** (n.) _____ was necessary since his was an online photography course, and he needed the ability to transfer large files with images without encountering too much **(3)** (n.) _____.

The orientation class at the beginning of the semester helped prevent many problems such as **(4)** (n.)_____ so that he could download lectures with steaming video. Also, he learned in the session how to participate in **(5)** (adj.)_____ whiteboard discussions during specified times as well as ways to meet with his professor during virtual office hours.

Learning to send **(6)** (n.) _____ through a **(7)** (adj.) _____ route was more complicated than he first thought. Again, however, the orientation session before the first day of class helped a great deal. It was during that session he learned some basic information about the **(8)** (n.) _____ of a computer as well as the proper language so he could follow computer protocol and get the good results the first time. The advances in technology impressed Norm, especially when he realized his school had wireless networks for the **(9)** (n.) _____ of students with laptops and **(10)** (n.) _____ for people who wanted to talk to each other during Internet meetings. The new technology made it possible for him to take more classes both online and face-to-face. As a result, he was optimistic about earning his degree and starting a new career in two years.

Stop and Think

 Pyramid Summary: Choose two words from this chapter and complete the pyramid summaries below. You may consult your dictionary or go to **www.dictionary.reference.com** and **www.etymonline.com** for additional help. Then compare your pyramids with a partner.

1. Word   **2.** Synonym   **3.** Antonym   **4.** Etymology   **5.** Sentence

1. _____

2. _____

3. _____

4. _____

5. _____

1. _____

2. _____

3. _____

4. _____

5. _____

 Using one of the words from the chapter, write a caption for the photograph.

_____

_____

_____

_____

_____

_____

_____

Vocabulary and Computer Technology

Get Ready to Read About Computer Technology

Computer technology textbooks contain topics such as the history and background of computer use, the Internet, networking, fiber optics, browsers, search engines, instant messaging, cookies, and streaming media. Also, new topics appear as the technology develops. Before you read this selection, consider what you already know about the following word parts. The meanings of some have been provided. Recall what you learned in Chapter 1 and fill in the blanks for the others.

The prefix *in-* means _____.

The prefix *inter-* means _____.

The suffix *-tion* means _____ and usually indicates a _____.

forum	innovation	mainstay	rapport	thread
hub	interface	post	solicit	upgrade

INFOPOP AND THE ULTIMATE
BULLETIN BOARD

The humble message board—one of the early **innovations** of the Internet in the 1970s and still one of the most popular—has been transformed in the last few years. Originally used by small groups to establish self-organizing communities around discussion topics, today, the message board is a **mainstay** of Fortune 1000 corporations who use message board technology to establish **rapport** with their customers. Now powered by high-end database management systems, today's boards can support up to 4 million page views a day, track discussion **threads,** and generate useful statistics on the content of messages for corporate marketers.

What do the *Financial Times*, Weather.com, BET.com, the Online Bible College, and the *Chronicle of the Horse* have in common? They all offer online communities powered by Infopop, one of the pioneers of bulletin board technology. Infopop began in 1996 when Ted O'Neill, the founder and CEO, released the first version of his Ultimate Bulletin Board (UBB) software as freeware. UBB allowed Web sites to offer a message board where users could participate in online discussions with one another. It proved so popular that O'Neill formed a company to release a licensed version. Customer feedback was **solicited,** the product improved, and the second version was released in December 1997. In 1998, UBB was **upgraded** several more times to allow multiple **forums** and the ability to add e-mail links, image links, hyperlinks, and customized code on most pages. New discussion moderator and administrative features and a search engine were also added. E-mail viewing for registered users, custom title graphics, and an announcement feature for moderators added to the success of the product, which at the beginning of 1999 was being used on over 90,000 Web sites. By 2003, that number had reached over 300,000 Web sites. Today, UBB enables users with small-to-medium sized Web sites to create a **hub** for online discussions. The downloadable software with a browser-based control panel allows Web sites to sort forum threads on pages separate from other Web site content. The unique customizable **interface** allows for a more fluid natural conversation with discussions divided up by forums on unlimited topics. Everyone can participate in the conversations, all members can view all **posts**, and private messaging is also available.

—Adapted from Laudon/Traver, *E-commerce: Business, Technology, Society,* p. 838. © 2004 Kenneth Laudon & Carol Traver. Reproduced by permission of Pearson Education, Inc. All rights reserved.

VISUAL VOCABULARY

Students today enjoy the _____ of computers and a variety of new programs that enhance their educational experience.

   a. hub
   b. innovation

Susan Pongratz

EXERCISE **1** Context Clues

Refer to the previous passage and use context clues from the sentences below to determine the definition of each of the following words in **bold** print. Do not consult a dictionary.

  1. forum (fôr′əm) n.
    In a recent public **forum**, the voters explained their opposition to widening the road.

    _____ **Forum** means
      a. play.   c. session.
      b. ballot.   d. opportunity.

  2. hub (hŭb) n.
    Although we were new to the city, we quickly discovered the **hub** where everyone gathered for good music and food in the evenings.

    _____ **Hub** means
      a. edge.   c. bottom.
      b. center.   d. boredom.

  3. innovation (ĭn′ə-vā′shən) n.
    When computers were first introduced in the 1940s for weather tracking and military operation, they were considered an obscure **innovation** and few predicted they would someday be a useful household item.

    _____ **Innovation** means
      a. reason.   c. decade.
      b. invitation.   d. invention.

4. interface (ĭn′tər-fās′) n.

   An efficient office needs a good **interface** between the office computers and the printers so that daily business runs smoothly.

   _____ **Interface** means

       a. interconnection.   c. benefit.
       b. payment.   d. delay.

5. mainstay (mān′stā′) n.

   During World War II when so many men were sent overseas, women became the **mainstay** of the workforce on the home front.

   _____ **Mainstay** means

       a. foundation.   c. soldier.
       b. series.   d. problem.

6. post (pōst) n.

   In a distance learning class, students are required to write a response and then reply to at least one other **post** that another student has made.

   _____ **Post** means

       a. wall.   c. recreation.
       b. message.   d. fence.

7. rapport (ră-pôr′) n.

   President Nichol's **rapport** with the students was obvious as he tossed a football with some freshmen in the Sunken Garden on the last day of classes.

   _____ **Rapport** means

       a. course.   c. close connection.
       b. fear.   d. disappointment.

8. solicit (sə-lĭs′ĭt) v.

   If you sign up at the "Do Not Call" registry, then telemarketers are no longer allowed to **solicit** sales from you.

   _____ **Solicit** means

       a. give.   c. provide.
       b. seek.   d. judge.

9. thread (thrĕd) n.

"After everyone has had a chance to post a response and reply to other students' comments," announced our professor, "the **thread** at the discussion board will be removed and a new one will be posted."

_____ **Thread** means
a. image.
b. fake site.
c. message series.
d. external link.

10. upgrade (ŭp'grād') v.

Periodically, automatic updates will **upgrade** the operating system on your computer to protect it from new viruses and keep it running smoothly.

_____ **Upgrade** means
a. seek.
b. ignore.
c. harm.
d. improve.

EXERCISE 2 Word Sorts

Synonyms

Match the word to the synonyms or definitions that follow each blank.

1. _____ message; response; reply; answer

2. _____ point of communication with computer and something else such as a printer; interconnection; layer between two boundaries

3. _____ foundation; support; backbone; reinforcement

4. _____ series; succession; string; line

5. _____ arena; panel; session; symposium

Antonyms

Select the letter of the word with the opposite meaning.

_____ **6.** rapport
a. alienation b. camaraderie c. connection d. understanding.

_____ **7.** innovation
a. invention b. intention c. antique d. reception

_____ **8.** hub
a. center b. focus c. point of departure d. border

_____ **9.** upgrade
   a. destroy   b. improve   c. develop   d. refine

_____ **10.** solicit
   a. propose   b. command   c. ask   d. share

EXERCISE **3** Fill in the Blank

Use context clues to determine the word that best completes each sentence.

1. If you _____ an existing program, you can spend less on the improvement than it would cost to purchase the latest version.

2. Incoming freshmen at a well-known university were recently given iPods in an effort to determine how the _____ could be adapted to an academic setting.

3. Several Internet sites provide _____ for questions and discussions on literary topics that are similar to those professors ask on essay exams.

4. An effective coach establishes _____ with the players, and that bonding inspires each person to work harder with the team.

5. To get enough protein, many vegetarians have beans and nuts as a _____ in their diets.

6. "Before you select a book for your project," said our professor, "you may want to go online and read a summary as well as the _____ by readers who offer their ratings of the title."

7. The human relations department serves as the _____ between employees and the state, thus interpreting and communicating employment policies to the workers.

8. Following his controversial editorial, the writer's website was jammed with a _____ of angry comments blasting his ideas.

9. Instead of doing everything alone, a good leader _____ the help of talented workers and then delegates certain responsibilities.

10. Chicago's O'Hare Airport is a major _____; its central location makes it ideal for connecting flights across the country.

EXERCISE 4 Application

Using context clues, insert the vocabulary word in the appropriate blank. A part-of-speech clue is given for each vocabulary word.

Over a period of several weeks, Emily had become interested in Nate, one of her classmates in a distance learning course. When she learned that he kept a blog, she knew it might be a chance for her to get to know him through the **(1)** (n.) _____ of this online journal. They both shared one online philosophy class, and she was impressed with the responses he posted to the **(2)** (n.) _____ in the discussion **(3)** (n.) _____ when Dr. Elder would **(4)** (v.) _____ comments and solutions for scenarios on ethics. Although the minimum requirement for each assignment was to write at least two **(5)** (n.) _____ for each response, Nate frequently participated with more replies.

In a recent discussion forum, Nate mentioned a foreign film he had viewed on his computer. However, when Emily tried to access it from her laptop in her dorm room, she realized she did not have enough bandwidth, so the video seemed choked by the Internet congestion coming into her dormitory. For that reason, the visual was like a jerky old home movie rather than the fluid projection she needed to follow the story line. Until she could **(6)** (v.) _____ her computer and improve the **(7)** (n.) _____ with the network so the connection was faster in her room, she would have to access the Internet someplace else for streaming video. She made a note to check out the film on one of the library's computers instead, since the new wireless network connection there was more rapid and much smoother. She had also learned that she could try telephony there, the college's new feature for having conversations over distances—something her class was planning to try as a discussion group before the end of the semester. Someday, that would be the **(8)** (n.) _____ of online courses instead of just the asynchronous discussion threads.

Emily liked studying in the library anyway. Just inside the library entrance was a coffee shop, which was the **(9)** (n.) _____ of many studious discussions, similar to those her class held online. Since the atmosphere was very casual, she could drop in, sit and listen, and occasionally ask a question or add a comment. With professors and students alike meeting there, it had become an extension of their classroom education. And since she read in Nate's blog that he liked to frequent the coffee shop on Thursday nights, this seemed to be a good place to begin a new friendship and establish **(10)** (n.) _____ with a classmate. If only she knew what he looked like!

Stop and Think

 Complete the following sentences based on the information provided.

1. Examples of some recent computer **innovations** are _____
   _____.

2. Telemarketers who **solicit** sales over the phone are _____
   _____.

3. If I could create a **hub** on my college campus it would include
   _____.

4. A **mainstay** of a college student's diet includes _____
   _____.

5. It is important to have **rapport** with _____
   _____.

Connect the following words to each of the pictures: **post, forum, upgrade, interface, thread.** Then support your choice by writing a sentence for each photograph using the word.

Word	Sentence
Courtesy of Microsoft.	1.
Courtesy of Microsoft.	2.
Courtesy of Microsoft.	3.
Courtesy of Microsoft.	4.
Courtesy of Microsoft.	5.

Review Test
Chapters 13–17

1 Word Parts

Match the definitions in Column 2 to the word parts in Column 1.

Column 1	Column 2
_____ **1.** equ	a. light
_____ **2.** fin	b. sound
_____ **3.** lum	c. far
_____ **4.** bio	d. equal; fair
_____ **5.** eco	e. life
_____ **6.** polis	f. city
_____ **7.** infra-	g. end
_____ **8.** syn-	h. same
_____ **9.** tele-	i. house; dwelling
_____ **10.** phon	j. underneath

4

2 Fill in the Blank

Use context clues to determine the best word from the box to complete each sentence.

ecosystem	forum	innovation	mainstay	radius
factor	hub	interface	post	solicit

1. It is an act of courage when we are humble enough to admit we cannot do something alone and are willing to _____ the help of others.

2. Part of a college education requires that students learn to participate in a variety of discussion _____ to share ideas.

3. Although our professor recognized academic freedom, he said that our online _____ for the class should be composed so that even our mothers would be proud to read them.

4. When we lost our network connection, the first thing we checked were the connecting wires leading into the _____.

5. Because NASA researchers had _____ in the safety aspects of the *Apollo 13* lunar module, the astronauts were saved, even though the mission was scrapped.

6. In addition to water, the _____ of any hiker's diet is protein.

7. The interesting part of a(n) _____, an area that contains living things, is that it can be as large as a forest or desert or as small as a droplet of water.

8. When he set up his new office, Chris ran wires so that his new computer would _____ with his printer, which was on the other side of the room.

9. One new _____ in Australia is the office building sleep pod where workers can take a 20-minute power nap while listening to music.

10. The landscape architect measured the _____ of the proposed circular driveway to determine how to arrange the new plants.

3 Book Connection

Use context clues to determine the best word from the box to complete each sentence. A part-of-speech clue is provided for each vocabulary word.

circuitous	dwindle	infinite	laden	mobility
distinctive	formula	pi	luminous	synchronous

THE SECRET LIFE OF BEES

During the summer of 1964, Lily Owens escapes from her life with an abusive father, a South Carolina peach farmer. When Lily was only four years old, her mother was killed, and Mr. Owens daily fuels Lily's pain over the loss by making her feel responsible for the death. For most of her life, Lily felt trapped, with little **(1)** (n.) _____ or freedom. The question of her role in her mother's death remained ever-present, however, because some details of that day are no longer **(2)** (adj.) _____ in her memory. In fact, the only memory she has of her mother is the day she died.

Age fourteen was a time when she should be memorizing algebra **(3)** (n.) _____ or learning about the mathematical application of **(4)** (n.) _____ to determine the circumference of a circle or developing crushes on the local high school baseball players. For Lily, though, life is almost unbearable with her father T-Ray—especially since the only unconditional love Lily experiences is from Rosaleen, a black woman who helps care for her and who exhibits the **(5)** (adj.) _____ love she should have experienced from her father. Lily's life begins to take a turn, however, when Rosaleen is arrested as a result of defying a pre-Civil Rights Act ruling: she tries to register to vote.

For both of them, hope rapidly **(6)** (v.) _____, until Lily decides what they have to do is *leave*. Together, they escape and travel a

4

(7) (adj.) _____ route to avoid the law and head toward Tibourn, South Carolina. There they find themselves in the midst of three unusual African American beekeeping sisters. They also experience **(8)** (adj.) _____, glowing, love-filled moments. It is also a time when Lily helps harvest honey from the bee hives that are **(9)** (adj.) _____ with nectar that becomes a metaphor for life. The **(10)** (adj.) _____ rhythm of the bee farm provides order and answers until another unthinkable event occurs in their lives.

The Secret Life of Bees has received national praise. A coming-of-age story with the same journey theme as many great books, it also focuses on betrayal, forgiveness, redemption, and love.

4 Visual Connection

Write a caption for this picture using two of the words in the box.

component	data	latency	signify	telephony
contiguous	derivative	molten	summit	variable

_____

_____

_____

_____

_____

_____

_____

_____

5 Analogies

Choose the word that best completes the analogy.

1. money : deposit :: venom : _____
   a. moderate   b. secrete   c. signify

2. engine : muffle :: voice : _____
   a. moderate   b. secrete   c. signify

3. subway : transportation:: underground cable : _____
   a. ecosystem   b. infrastructure   c. bandwidth

4. mile : yard :: kilometer : _____
   a. inch   b. foot   c. meter

5. words : conversation :: response : _____
   a. computer   b. thread   c. board

6. house: remodel :: computer : _____
   a. signify   b. solicit   c. upgrade

7. line : angle :: curve : _____
   a. arc   b. meter   c. post

8. water : flood :: snow : _____
   a. rivulet   b. ecosystem   c. avalanche

9. soda : straw :: frequency : _____
   a. bandwidth   b. post   c. formula

10. words : sentence :: numbers : _____
    a. radius   b. variable   c. equation

UNIT 5 Vocabulary in Communication and Humanities

Vocabulary and Interpersonal Communication

Get Ready to Read About Interpersonal Communication

College is a good place to learn how to communicate more effectively. Many students are required to take a course in interpersonal communication, which is the study of how we relate to ourselves and others through what we say, how we say it, and what we leave unsaid. This course explores the power of words as well as body language. Before you read this selection, recall what you already know about the following word parts. The meanings of some have been provided. Recall what you learned in Chapter 1 and fill in the blanks for the others.

1. The prefix *dis-* means _____ or *separated from*.

2. The prefix *in-* means *not* or *into*.

3. The prefix *inter-* means _____.

4. The prefix *pre-* means _____.

5. The root *fid-* means *faith.*

6. The suffix *-able* means _____ and indicates an adjective.

7. The suffix *-ate* means _____ and indicates a verb.

8. The suffix *-ity* means *quality* or *trait* and indicates a noun.

9. The suffix *-ment* means *act* or *state* and indicates a noun.

10. The suffix *-tion* means _____ and indicates a noun.

| accumulate | disclose | infidelity | interaction | precipitate |
| deterioration | incremental | infringement | intolerable | tenuous |

HOW RELATIONSHIPS END

A declining relationship usually follows one of several paths. Sometimes a relationship loses steam and runs down like a dying battery. Instead of a single event that causes the breakup, the relationship fades away—the two partners just drift further and further apart, and the relationship becomes more **tenuous**. They spend less time together, let more time go by between **interactions,** and stop **disclosing** much about themselves. You've probably had a number of friendships that ended this way—perhaps long-distance relationships. Long-distance relationships require a great deal of effort to maintain, so a move can easily decrease the level of intimacy.

Some relationships end in sudden death. As the name suggests, sudden death moves straight to separation. One partner might move away or die, or more frequently, a single precipitating event such as **infidelity,** breaking a confidence, a major conflict, or some other major role **infringement precipitates** the breakup. Sudden death is like taking an express elevator from a top floor to ground level.

In between fading away and sudden death lies incrementalism. Incrementalism is the process by which conflicts and problems continue to **accumulate** in the relationship until they reach a critical mass that leads to the **deterioration** of the breakup; the relationship becomes **intolerable** or, from a social exchange perspective, too costly. "I just got to a point where it wasn't worth it anymore" and "It got to the point where all we did was fight all the time" are typical statements about **incremental** endings.

—Adapted from Steven A. Beebe, Susan J. Beebe, and Mark V. Redmond, *Interpersonal Communication: Relating to Others,* 3e, pp. 344-345. Published by Allyn and Bacon, Boston, MA. Copyright © 2002 by Pearson Education. Reprinted by permission of the publisher.

VISUAL VOCABULARY

During the 18th century, pirates sailed the Caribbean waters in search of treasure and committing

_____ acts such as stealing ships and their cargo.

   a. intolerable
   b. incremental

George Pongratz

EXERCISE 1 Context Clues

Refer to the previous passage and use context clues from the sentences below to determine the definition of each of the following words in **bold** print. Do not consult a dictionary.

1. accumulate (ə-kyo͞om′yə-lāt′) v.
A travel advisory was issued as the unexpected snowfall was predicted to **accumulate** to more than 12 inches.

_____ **Accumulate** means
   a. pile up.   c. decrease.
   b. lessen.   d. imagine.

2. deterioration (dĭ-tēr′ē-ə-rā′shən) n.
The **deterioration** of Adam's grades first started when his girlfriend unexpectedly broke up with him, but he quickly realized he needed to refocus his attention to finish the semester successfully.

_____ **Deterioration** means
   a. condition of improving.   c. process of becoming boring.
   b. condition of becoming worse.   d. process of showing excellence.

3. disclose (dĭ-sklōz′) v.
Before selling, homeowners are required by law to **disclose** anything they know that is wrong with the property or dwelling.

_____ **Disclose** means
   a. seal.   c. understand.
   b. hide.   d. reveal.

4. incremental (ĭn'krə-mĕn'tl) adj.
Because he knew how a savings account can increase in **incremental** amounts over many years, Einstein once said, "The most powerful force in the universe is compounding interest."

_____ **Incremental** means
  a. decreasing quickly.
  b. increasing gradually.
  c. rising suddenly.
  d. a sudden drop.

5. infidelity (ĭn'fĭ-dĕl'ĭ-tē) n.
The popular Hollywood couple announced their separation during a flurry of publicity, and although they did not give a reason, most believed it was because of the husband's **infidelity** with his most recent leading lady.

_____ **Infidelity** means
  a. honesty.
  b. popularity.
  c. unfaithfulness.
  d. public performance.

6. infringement (ĭn-frĭnj'mənt) n.
Because they viewed it as an **infringement** of constitutional rights, many public officials were outraged when they discovered the Patriot Act gave the government wiretapping permission to listen in on the conversations of private citizens.

_____ **Infringement** means
  a. observance.
  b. good deed.
  c. obedience.
  d. violation.

7. interaction (ĭn'tər-ăk'shən) n.
Often during a job interview, candidates will be invited to lunch so that they can be observed during their **interaction** with future co-workers.

_____ **Interaction** means
  a. communication.
  b. loneliness.
  c. weak force.
  d. opposition.

8. intolerable (ĭn-tŏl'ər-ə-bəl) adj.
When colonists decided that British rule had become **intolerable**, they plotted the beginnings of a revolution.

_____ **Intolerable** means
  a. desirable.
  b. unbearable.
  c. acceptable.
  d. unsure.

9. precipitate (prĭ-sĭp′ĭ-tāt′) v.
Encouragement from Ted's art teachers **precipitated** a switch in his major from civil engineering to fine arts.

_____ **Precipitate** means

a. cause.   c. avoid.

b. stop.   d. open.

10. tenuous (tĕn′yōō-əs) adj.
When Lindsay's political science professor read her persuasive essay, he said it needed more work because it was filled with opinions with only **tenuous** support, causing it to sound like a feeble argument.

_____ **Tenuous** means

a. strong.   c. weak.

b. convincing.   d. valuable.

EXERCISE 2 Word Sorts

Synonyms

Match the word to the synonyms or definitions that follow each blank.

1. _____ correspondence; communication; interchange; interconnection

2. _____ unbearable; unacceptable; insufferable; painful

3. _____ in a manner of gradual increase; in a manner of slow augmentation

4. _____ trigger; bring on; hasten; push forward

5. _____ shaky; weak; fragile; unsubstantiated

Antonyms

Select the letter of the word(s) with the opposite meaning.

_____ 6. accumulate

a. acquire   b. pass   c. possess   d. lose

_____ 7. deterioration

a. improvement b. crumbling   c. destruction d. disappearance

_____ 8. disclose

a. reveal   b. hide   c. gather   d. trespass

_____ **9.** infringement
a. obedience   b. explanation   c. honor   d. misbehavior

_____ **10.** infidelity
a. unfaithfulness   b. faithfulness   c. secret   d. gossip

EXERCISE 3 Fill in the Blank

Use context clues to determine the word that best completes each sentence.

1. Once he moved to another state, Eric sadly realized his relationship with Randi, his college girlfriend, would become too _____ to sustain over the long distance.

2. The sudden turn in favor of the home team _____ a roar of cheers from local fans.

3. Because the college's star quarterback had _____ a number of legal infractions as well as unsportsmanlike offenses, he was suspended from the team.

4. When Maya learned of her boyfriend's _____ with a stranger at a fraternity party, she had to make a decision whether to forgive him or end their relationship.

5. On graduation day, the two best friends vowed not to let distance cause the _____ of their friendship, even though they would be working in different states.

6. Financial advisors stress that bonds are long-term investments because the increase in funds occurs in _____ steps over many years.

7. When running for public office, a candidate is required to _____ all sources of funds received for the campaign.

8. Until the age of three, most children do not have much _____ with other children; rather, they participate in what is known as "parallel play" in which they play alone alongside another child.

9. The language in the film was so offensive and _____ that Sarah and her boyfriend left midway through the movie without even asking for a refund.

10. Opponents of hidden cameras in public areas argue that they are an _____ of a citizen's civil liberties.

EXERCISE **4** Application

Using context clues, insert the vocabulary word in the appropriate blank. A part-of-speech clue is given for each vocabulary word.

Stunned, Amy stared at the e-mail from her boyfriend Derrick and felt numb as she reread his confession, which **(1)** (v.) _____ that he was no longer interested in dating her. There was no act of **(2)** (n.) _____—no unfaithfulness on his part—to **(3)** (v.) _____ the writing of the letter. Instead, it seems he was, well, bored, and that their relationship was becoming more **(4)** (adj.) _____.

Actually, this fact would not surprise sociologists who study the **(5)** (n.) _____ of college students. The main reason for the **(6)** (n.) _____ of college couples' relationships is usually a lack of interest, rather than some **(7)** (adj.) _____ and horrible event.

Predictably, Amy felt betrayed at first. She felt there had been an **(8)** (n.) _____ of the closeness she and Derrick had developed. However, after more reflection, Amy began to think of the good things about their breakup. For one, she could once again pursue her own interests and begin to make new memories. She could allow herself to be selfish and do things she enjoyed.

To overcome her sadness, the first thing Amy did was to remove all souvenirs, photos, and letters that she had **(9)** (v.) _____. But instead of throwing them away, she put them in a box on the top shelf of her closet. Then she worked at developing some mental discipline by training her thoughts to think of the future with a hopeful outlook. She knew enough about psychology to know that her success would be **(10)** (adj.) _____; however, her mother had taught her, "Little by little does the trick." For that reason, she decided to face each day with a more hopeful outlook, ready for the new adventures and new people ahead.

Stop and Think

Fill in the blanks with words from the chapter to summarize the interpersonal communication textbook passage.

_____

_____

_____

Consult your collegiate dictionary or go to **www.dictionary.com** or **www.merriam-webster.com** to determine other forms of the words from the chapter.

Noun	Verb	Adjective	Adverb
_____	accumulate	_____	_____
deterioration	_____	_____	_____
_____	disclose	_____	_____
_____		incremental	_____
infringement	_____		
interaction	_____	_____	_____
_____	precipitate	_____	_____

Vocabulary and Intercultural Communication

Get Ready to Read About Intercultural Communication

A specialized branch of interpersonal communication is intercultural communication, which provides a global view of how people receive and send messages to each other. This course also helps people understand the communication differences among cultures. Before you read this selection, consider what you already know about the following word parts. The meanings of some have been provided. Recall what you learned in Chapter 1 and fill in the blanks for the others.

1. The prefix *ambi-* means *both*.

2. The prefix *em-* means *within*.

3. The prefix *inter-* means _____.

4. The root *ethno* means *people, nation, class*.

5. The root *phob* means _____.

6. The root *xeno* means *stranger*.

7. The suffix *-al* means *like, of, related to* and indicates an _____.

8. The suffix *-ic* means _____ and indicates an _____.

9. The suffix *-ism* means *belief* and indicates a _____.

| ambiguity | augment | ethnocentrism | intercultural | tolerate |
| assumption | empathic | hamper | stereotype | xenophobia |

INTERCULTURAL COMMUNICATION

Intercultural communication occurs when individuals or groups from different cultures communicate. Several barriers inhibit effective intercultural communication. **Ethnocentrism** is the belief that one's own cultural traditions and **assumptions** are superior to those of others. Differences in language and the way people interpret nonverbal messages also interfere with effective intercultural communication and can encourage **xenophobia**, fear and distrust of strangers. People **stereotype** by placing a group or a person into an inflexible, all-encompassing category. A related barrier is prejudice—people often prejudge someone before they know all the facts. Stereotyping and prejudice can keep people from viewing others as unique individuals and therefore **hamper** effective, honest communication. Finally, assuming that one is similar to others can also be a barrier to intercultural communication. All humans have some similarities, but their cultures have taught them to process the world differently.

Although it is reasonably easy to identify cultural differences, it is more challenging to bridge those differences. To enhance understanding between cultures, we suggest the following: Develop knowledge by seeking information about the culture, ask questions, and listen and develop a "third culture." Increase your motivation to appreciate others who are different from you by **tolerating ambiguity,** developing mindfulness, and avoiding negative judgments about another culture. Finally, **augment** your skill by becoming more flexible. Be other-oriented by socially decentering and becoming more **empathic**. And adapt your verbal and nonverbal communication to others.

VISUAL VOCABULARY

Reading provides opportunities to

_____ our knowledge about many areas of life.

   a. augment
   b. stereotype

George Pongratz

EXERCISE 1 Context Clues

Refer to the previous passage and use context clues from the sentences below to determine the definition of each of the following words in **bold** print. Do not consult a dictionary.

1. ambiguity (ăm′bĭ-gyoo′ĭ-tē) n.
The supervisor's report had to be rewritten because of a major **ambiguity** that made the paper unclear, thus creating confusion in the board meeting.

   _____ **Ambiguity** means
     a. uncertainty.   c. sureness.
     b. hope.   d. cooperation.

2. assumption (ə-sŭmp′shən) n.
Since she did not know how long the essay should be, Anna worked on the **assumption** that her teacher wanted quality rather than quantity.

   _____ **Assumption** means
     a. withdrawal.   c. fall.
     b. expectation.   d. rejection.

3. augment (ôg-mĕnt′) v.
When we **augment** our personal vocabulary, we are also increasing our background knowledge, which makes learning new information easier.

   _____ **Augment** means
     a. add to.   c. confuse.
     b. take away.   d. surround.

4. empathic (ĕm-păth´ĭk) adj.
   Because of her **empathic** nature, people seek out Alexis for advice and a sympathetic ear.

   _____ **Empathic** means
       a. nasty.   c. caring.
       b. unfriendly.   d. close-minded.

5. ethnocentrism (ĕth´nō-sĕn´trĭz´əm) n.
   In Spanish class, we were assigned a project to learn about several Spanish-speaking cultures to help reduce our tendency toward **ethnocentrism**, always believing that the American way is the best.

   _____ **Ethnocentrism** means
       a. belief in the superiority of one's own group.
       b. belief in joining a political party.
       c. belief in a two-party system.
       d. belief in many gods.

6. hamper (hăm´pər) v.
   We had planned to arrive at the mountain cabin in two hours; however, the rain **hampered** driving conditions, which doubled the travel time.

   _____ **Hamper** means
       a. interfere.   c. encourage.
       b. help.   d. allow.

7. intercultural (ĭn´tər-kŭl´chər-əl) adj.
   The International Club on campus sponsors **intercultural** lectures by students from foreign countries who are willing to share information about their homeland.

   _____ **Intercultural** means
       a. relating to many generations.
       b. relating to art.
       c. relating to many different cultures.
       d. relating to many different species.

8. stereotype (stĕr´ē-ə-tīp´) v.
   It's very hard not to **stereotype** people if you have had limited experience meeting those outside your own community of friends.

   _____ **Stereotype** means
       a. copy.   c. ignore.
       b. file.   d. categorize.

9. tolerate (tŏl'ə-rāt') v.

When asked his secret of success, baseball legend Reggie Jackson said that he felt it was important to learn to endure failure but not to **tolerate** it.

_____ **Tolerate** means
   a. accept.   c. give in to.
   b. disapprove.   d. veto.

10. xenophobia (zĕn'ə-fō'bē-ə) n.

When Mohammed and his parents moved to a new neighborhood, they patiently waited for the residents to overcome their **xenophobia**; eventually the neighbors shed their suspicions and began to trust Mohammed's family.

_____ **Xenophobia** means
   a. fear of superheroes.   c. fear of xylophones.
   b. fear of clowns.   d. fear of strangers.

EXERCISE 2 Word Sorts

Synonyms

Match the word to the synonyms or definitions that follow each blank.

1. _____ of or relating to different cultures

2. _____ fear of strangers; narrowness; discrimination

3. _____ the belief that one's culture is the best

4. _____ sensitive; compassionate; responsive

5. _____ generalize; universalize; label

Antonyms

Select the letter of the word(s) with the opposite meaning.

_____ **6.** ambiguity
       a. unclearness   b. certainty   c. doubt   d. mistrust

_____ **7.** tolerate
       a. discuss   b. hold down   c. restrict   d. condemn

_____ **8.** assumption
       a. truth   b. belief   c. sample   d. concern

_____ **9.** augment
       a. surround   b. include   c. leave   d. exclude

_____ **10.** hamper
       a. hinder   b. restrict   c. promote   d. cover

EXERCISE 3 Fill in the Blank

Use context clues to determine the word that best completes each sentence.

1. To _____ city revenue, the council decided to raise the property assessments by 25 percent.

2. After studying all sides of the issue, Richard was able to _____ and accept the two views of the problem.

3. Traveling to France, Spain, and Italy gave Barbara an _____ experience.

4. Because of an _____ in the contract, Tina refused to sign the papers until her lawyer could negotiate terms that were more clearly stated.

5. Although many people _____ plumbers, making the generalization that they are not intellectuals, Amanda discovered that hers was a published poet.

6. At the beginning of the trial, the judge cautioned the jury to avoid making any _____ about the defendant and recognize that he was innocent until proven guilty.

7. A weak vocabulary can _____ reading speed and restrict comprehension.

8. Of all the excessive fears people experience, _____ is one that also touches the strangers and foreigners who are mistrusted.

9. An interesting example of _____ is food preferences that prevent individuals from trying something new and make them believe only familiar recipes are the best.

10. Kat's _____ personality and love of nature prevent her from enjoying any films that involve injury to animals.

EXERCISE 4 Application

Using context clues, insert the vocabulary word in the appropriate blank. A part-of-speech clue is given for each vocabulary word.

When Sana first arrived in this country, she was careful about meeting people on her college campus because she had heard that Americans had a tendency to **(1)** (v.) _____ and form judgments because of how someone looked. In her case, she worried that someone would make unfair **(2)** (n.) _____ about her based on her speech; thus her heavy accent prevented her willingness to talk with others. In addition, her natural shyness also **(3)** (v.) _____ her ability to make new friends.

What Sana soon discovered, however, was that **(4)** (n.) _____ was rare on most college campuses. Indeed, fear of strangers and foreigners did not usually occur in the academic world because college students long to know more about the diversity of the world. In fact, students seek out people from other countries and even sign up for study-abroad programs in order to have an **(5)** (adj.) _____ experience.

Sana finally began to make friends when she joined the International Club, an organization in which students share information about their homelands to clear up misinformation and any **(6)** (n.) _____ about another country. Hence, education decreases **(7)** (n.) _____, so that people no longer think of their country's method as the one and only way. Instead, students become more **(8)** (adj.) _____, sharing a sympathetic understanding of the world. They also receive an education that **(9)** (v.) _____ their knowledge beyond math or English or chemistry; they develop a global view. Consequently, they are able to **(10)** (v.) _____ differences and become more accepting of others' views.

Stop and Think

 Pyramid Summary: Fill in the lines below for the words *hamper* and *augment* so that each has at least three synonyms, four antonyms, and one sentence using the word.

1. _____

_____

_____

_____

2. _____

_____

_____

_____

 Complete the table with other forms of the words from this chapter. You may need to consult a dictionary or **www.dictionary.com**

Noun	Verb	Adjective
ambiguity		_____
assumption	_____	
_____	_____	empathic
_____	stereotype	_____
_____	tolerate	_____

Vocabulary and Art History

Get Ready to Read About Art History

Humanities is a group of courses that explore the human condition and include subjects such as religion, philosophy, architecture, music appreciation, literature, and art history—all of which require a great deal of memorization. In art history, students do well if they have a strong background knowledge of history and the ability to notice details.

Before you read this selection, recall what you already know about the following word parts. The meanings of some have been provided. Recall what you learned in Chapter 1 and fill in the blanks for the others.

1. The prefix *re-* means _____.

2. The root *arch* means _____ or _____.

3. The root *mur* means *wall*.

4. The root *nasci* means *to be born*.

5. The suffix *-ate* means _____ and indicates a _____.

6. The suffix *-ist* means *one who specializes* and indicates a

   _____.

7. The suffix *-ize* means *cause to become* and indicates a _____.

| accord | celebrate | futurist | mechanized | pioneering |
| architecture | epitomize | groundwork | mural | Renaissance |

LEONARDO DA VINCI

The **pioneering groundwork** for the **mechanized** world of the future lay in the fantastic imaginings of Leonardo da Vinci (1452–1519), who would be famous if all he had left behind were the portrait known as the *Mona Lisa* and the **mural** *The Last Supper.* His career, however, **epitomizes** everything we have come to label "**Renaissance,**" that amazing period of new art, music, **architecture,** and politics, beginning in the early fifteenth century and lasting for at least three hundred years.

Philosopher, poet, artist, **futurist**, and inventor, Leonardo da Vinci has been **accorded** by history that rarest of titles, *uomo universale.* He is widely **celebrated** as the creator of artistic masterpieces, but had he never painted his two most famous works, he could still claim his share of space in history books on the strength of his technology alone.

—From Richard Paul Janaro and Thelma C. Altshuler, *The Art of Being Human,* 6th Edition. New York: Longman, 2000, p. 49. Reprinted by permission of Pearson Education, Inc., Glenview, IL.

VISUAL VOCABULARY

The arch, one of the most famous forms in _____, can be seen in Roman aqueducts, the Eiffel Tower, and even in these windows from an ancient wall in London, England.

a. groundwork
b. architecture

Elizabeth Pongratz

EXERCISE **1** Context Clues

Refer to the previous passage and use context clues from the sentences below to determine the definition of each of the following words in **bold** print. Do not consult a dictionary.

1. accord (ə-kôrd´) v.

Following his term of office, Jimmy Carter started a new career and was eventually **accorded** the honor of the Nobel Peace Prize—proof that former presidents continue to have productive lives after their public service.

_____ **Accord** means

a. create.   c. argue.

b. give.   d. challenge.

2. architecture (är´kĭ-tĕk´chər) n.

The **architecture** of some cities such as London encompasses a variety of styles from ancient Roman to English Tudor to the very modern glass and steel "Eye of London," which is an impressive Ferris wheel.

_____ **Architecture** means

a. building destruction. c. room arrangement.

b. building design.   d. decoration.

3. celebrate (sĕl´ə-brāt´) v.

The Horatio Alger Society **celebrates** the accomplishments of Americans such as Oprah Winfrey, Benjamin Carson, and Walter Anderson, who began in humble surroundings and overcame great difficulties to achieve success in their field.

_____ **Celebrate** means

a. ignore.   c. praise.

b. forgive.   d. criticize.

4. epitomize (ĭ-pĭt´ə-mīz´) v.

Thomas Jefferson **epitomizes** the intellectual, the artist, the gentleman farmer, and the statesman.

_____ **Epitomize** means

a. recognize.   c. complain.

b. teach.   d. be an example of.

5. futurist (fyoo´chə-rĭst´) n.

Architect Frank Lloyd Wright was a **futurist** in his field, designing buildings and furniture that were far advanced for the time.

_____ **Futurist** means
a. one who imagines possibilities.
b. one who relies on the past.
c. person who works for a wealthy leader.
d. person who studies numbers.

6. groundwork (ground′wûrk′) n.
Before students can take calculus, they must demonstrate that they have a strong **groundwork** in algebra and geometry, since a secure foundation will help ensure they succeed.

_____ **Groundwork** means
a. misunderstanding.   c. imagination.
b. foundation.   d. tutoring session.

7. mechanized(měk′ə-nīzd′) adj.
As manufacturing became more **mechanized** and automated, fewer factory workers were needed and many areas of the country experienced an increase in the unemployment rate.

_____ **Mechanized** means
a. in charge.
b. added to.
c. equipped with machinery.
d. equipped with a protective covering.

8. mural (myoor′əl) n.
Our favorite Italian restaurant is decorated with **murals** of scenes from Florence, Rome, and Venice painted on one long wall.

_____ **Mural** means
a. principle of right and wrong.
b. information.
c. an important document.
d. large image painted directly on a wall.

9. pioneering (pī′ə-nîr′-ŋ) adj.
The Wright brothers are famous for their **pioneering** first flight in Kitty Hawk, North Carolina, which laid the foundation for future exploration in the field.

_____ **Pioneering** means
a. ground-breaking.   c. unoriginal.
b. traditional.   d. typical.

10. Renaissance (rĕn′ĭ-säns′) n.
The cultural rebirth of European history covers the period from the 1300s to the mid-1600s, a period known as the **Renaissance.**

_____ **Renaissance** means
a. revival of art and culture.   c. disappearance.
b. exit.   d. destruction of art and culture.

EXERCISE 2 Word Sorts

Synonyms

Match the word to the synonyms or definitions that follow each blank.

1. _____ visionary

2. _____ building design; building planning; building composition

3. _____ automated; computerized; automatic

4. _____ period of art revival that originated in 14th century Italy

5. _____ wall painting

Antonyms

Select the letter of the word(s) with the opposite meaning.

_____ **6.** accord
a. bestow   b. oppose   c. admit   d. send

_____ **7.** pioneering
a. unoriginal b. creative   c. reviving   d. developing

_____ **8.** groundwork
a. foundation b. reception   c. understructure d. top

_____ **9.** epitomize
a. refine   b. make clear c. define   d. confuse

_____ **10.** celebrate
a. ignore   b. instruct   c. surround   d. honor

EXERCISE 3 Fill in the Blank

Use context clues to determine the word that best completes each sentence.

1. William grew tired of the _____ world of computers, fax machines, and elevators, so he sold his business and bought a log cabin in the mountains.

2. Both roommates were fine arts majors; however, one specialized in painting miniature portraits while the other preferred creating huge _____ on the sides of buildings.

3. Stephanie considered herself a _____, but her boyfriend was a historian who preferred to live in the past.

4. The newly elected delegate held town meetings to lay the _____ for open communication between the government and private citizens.

5. An _____ major, Naomi often spent hours creating models of structures such as bus stops inspired by Stonehenge or movie theaters that looked like the Parthenon.

6. Marie and Pierre Curie collaborated on research in physics and were _____ the Nobel Prize in 1903.

7. Dr. Fontaine _____ the efficient, ambitious, capable business woman, and her constant aim for excellence inspires us all.

8. Always a gracious competitor, Ben _____ the victory of his opponent at the awards ceremony, acknowledging the race had been a challenge.

9. Ed Germain, noted NASA engineer, helped with the _____ plans of the first supersonic airplane piloted by Chuck Yeager.

10. In addition to Leonardo da Vinci, Michelangelo is probably the other most famous artist of the _____.

EXERCISE 4 Application

Using context clues, insert the vocabulary word in the appropriate blank. A part-of-speech clue is given for each vocabulary word.

Matt studied the assignment for his class in **(1)** (n.) _____, rereading the details of the building design he was to create for his final project. His teacher, a man who had been **(2)** (v.) _____ the title of "Professor of the Year" for three consecutive years, was someone Matt wanted to please, not only because his teacher was an artist who had been **(3)** (v.) _____ in his field, but also because Matt appreciated the man's genius and vision. In fact, his professor had been responsible for some **(4)** (adj.) _____ designs in the past, which had been recognized worldwide. If he could earn his professor's praise for the final project, Matt reasoned, then perhaps he could get a recommendation for an internship at a European firm where he could study ways to incorporate visionary designs for practical purposes. Matt's favorite period in art and architecture was the **(5)** (n.) _____, and he hoped to apply that style to new build- ings, thus preserving the beauty of the old world.

Matt knew of some architects who encompassed the designs of the 15th century into practical buildings—a technique he hoped to learn in order to decrease the world's fascination with the cheap, **(6)** (adj.) _____ shapes that some **(7)** (n.) _____ imagined and hoped to sell for potential construction opportunities. Matt's plan, however, was different. In his buildings, he wanted to incorporate artwork created by the masters who **(8)** (v.) _____ great art such as Leonardo da Vinci and Michelangelo. The use of sculptures, paintings, and even **(9)** (n.) _____ on the outside walls was part of his plan to teach the world to embrace the beauty of another time.

Because his professor had laid the **(10)** (n.) _____ for his vision of excellent work, Matt hoped he could follow through with a superior final project and make his teacher proud.

Stop and Think

 Use your dictionary or go to **http://thesaurus.reference.com** to fill in the other forms of the words below, and then write a synonym and sentence for each. For some, you may need to use the thesaurus feature at the website. Note that some categories will not have an answer.

Noun	Verb	Adjective
1._____ _____ _____	accord	
2._____ _____ _____ _____	celebrate	3. _____ used for celebrating: triumphant 2. After the soccer tournament, we were all in a celebratory mood.
4._____ _____ _____	epitomize	
futurist		5. _____ _____ _____ _____

 One-Word Summary: Go to **www.ibiblio.org/wm/paint/auth/vinci/joconde/** or **http://en.wikipedia.org/wiki/Mona_Lisa** and read about Leonardo da Vinci's *Mona Lisa*. Next, choose one vocabulary word from this chapter to summarize what you have learned about the painting and explain the reasons for your choice on your own paper.

CHAPTER

21

Vocabulary and Literature

Get Ready to Read About Literature

A part of the humanities curriculum, literature encompasses a variety of genres, or categories, such as the novel, short story, poetry, plays, and non-fiction essays.

Before you read this selection, recall what you already know about the following word parts. The meanings of some have been provided. Recall what you learned in Chapter 1 and fill in the blanks for the others.

1. The prefix *im-* means _____.

2. The prefix *per-* means _____.

3. The prefix *meta-* means *after, changed*, or *beyond*.

4. The root *belli* means _____.

5. The suffix *-ent* means *of, like, related* and usually indicates an

    _____.

6. The suffix *-ous* means *full of* and usually indicates an _____.

| belligerent | impart | perceive | sarcastic | tendril |
| hostile | metaphor | ponderous | taunt | tone |

TONE IN A POEM

In old Western movies, when one hombre **taunts** another, it is customary for the second to drawl, "Smile when you say that, pardner" or "Mister, I don't like your **tone** of voice." Sometimes in reading a poem, although we can neither see a face nor hear a voice, we can infer the poet's attitude from other evidence.

Like tone of voice, tone in literature often **imparts** an attitude toward the person addressed. Like the manner of a person, the manner of a poem may be friendly or **belligerent** toward its reader. Again like tone of voice, the tone of a poem may tell us how the speaker feels about himself or herself: cocksure or humble, sad or glad. But usually when we ask, "What is the tone of a poem?" we mean "What attitude does the poet take toward a theme or subject?" Is the poet being affectionate, **hostile**, earnest, playful, **sarcastic,** or what? We may never be able to know, of course, the poet's personal feelings. All we need know is how to feel when we read the poem.

Strictly speaking, tone isn't an attitude; it is whatever in the poem makes an attitude clear to us: the choice of words instead of others, the picking out of certain details. In A.E. Houseman's "Loveliest of Trees," for example, the poet communicates his admiration for a cherry tree's beauty by singing out for attention its white blossoms; had he wanted to show his dislike for the trees, he might have concentrated on its broken branches, birdlime, or snails. To **perceive** the tone of a poem correctly, we need to read the poem carefully, paying attention to whatever suggestions we find in it.

—Adapted from X. J. Kennedy and Dana Gioia, *Literature: An Introduction to Fiction, Poetry, and Drama*, 8th Edition. New York: Longman, 2002, p. 757. Reprinted by permission of Pearson Education, Inc., Glenview, IL.

Study the following poem by 20th century poet Sylvia Plath.

METAPHORS

I'm a riddle in nine syllables,
An elephant, a **ponderous** house,
A melon strolling on two **tendrils.**
O red fruit, ivory, fine timbers!
This loaf's big with its yeasty rising.
Money's new-minted in this fat purse.
I'm a means, a stage, a cow in calf.
I've eaten a bag of green apples,
Boarded the train there's no getting off.

—From *Crossing the Water* by Sylvia Plath. Copyright © 1960 by Ted Hughes. Reprinted by permission of HarperCollins Publishers and Faber and Faber Ltd.

VISUAL VOCABULARY

Because of their size, oxen often are referred to as

_____ animals.

  a. sarcastic
  b. ponderous

George Pongratz

EXERCISE 1 Context Clues

Refer to the previous passage and use context clues from the sentences below to determine the definition of each of the following words in **bold** print. Do not consult a dictionary.

1. belligerent (bə-lĭj′ər-ənt) adj.
Some pediatricians believe that spending an excessive amount of time playing violent video games may make children more **belligerent** and prone to use force to solve their problems.

  _____ **Belligerent** means
    a. peaceful.   c. overweight.
    b. inclined to fight.   d. passive.

2. hostile (hŏs′təl) adj.
The threat of a **hostile** takeover of the company sent many stockholders scrambling to sell their shares, which they feared would be devalued if the company was forced to merge with a larger firm.

  _____ **Hostile** means
    a. friendly.   c. aggressive.
    b. kind.   d. popular.

3. impart (ĭm-pärt′) v.

Benton could always count on his mother to **impart** wisdom with unconditional love.

_____ **Impart** means

a. take away.   c. receive.

b. share.   d. learn.

4. metaphor (mĕt′ə-fôr′) n.

In his novel *Fight Club*, Chuck Palahniuk uses the idea of a fight club as a **metaphor** for male bonding in the way women previously used a quilting group or book club for support.

_____ **Metaphor** means

a. comparison.   c. contrast.

b. difference.   d. memory.

5. perceive (pər-sēv′) v.

Although we may **perceive** nursery rhymes and songs as simple and fanciful, many are actually about war and politics, such as "La Cucaracha," which is about the Mexican Revolution.

_____ **Perceive** means

a. ignore.   c. neglect.

b. overlook.   d. understand.

6. ponderous (pŏn′dər-əs) adj.

When he returned from fighting in World War II, Bob traveled and camped across the country with a friend for an entire summer in order to shake off the **ponderous** and heavy feelings he had about all the tragedy he had seen in the Pacific.

_____ **Ponderous** means

a. light.   c. burdensome.

b. happy.   d. graceful.

7. sarcastic (sär-kăs′tĭk) adj.

When a stranger approached the brown-eyed, brown-haired couple and looked at their child with the blond hair, asking, "Who has blue eyes and blond hair," the mother answered in a **sarcastic** tone, "Brad Pitt."

_____ **Sarcastic** means

a. sweetly good-humored.   c. thoughtfully kind.

b. respectfully dignified. d. wittily sharp.

8. taunt (tônt) v.

Playground bullies who **taunt** quiet, shy children often have experienced the same verbal abuse at home.

_____ **Taunt** means

    a. tease.   c. praise.

    b. compliment.   d. please.

9. tendril (tĕn′drəl) n.

Ella's stylist piled curls on the top of her head but allowed a few loose **tendrils** to frame her face.

_____ **Tendril** means

    a. award.   c. question.

    b. playful attention.   d. thin coil.

10. tone (tōn) n.

Judging by the serious **tone** of his physics professor, Jeff predicted that the lab projects were disappointing.

_____ **Tone** means

    a. health.   c. body language.

    b. tint.   d. quality of a person's voice.

EXERCISE 2 Word Sorts

Synonyms

Match the word to the synonyms or definitions that follow each blank.

1. _____ a comparison of two unlike things without using the words _like_ or _as_

2. _____ tell; disclose; communicate

3. _____ attitude; inflection; mood

4. _____ understand; comprehend; recognize

5. _____ coil; curlicue; spiral

Antonyms

Select the letter of the word with the opposite meaning.

_____ **6.** taunt

    a. torment   c. encircle

    b. compliment   d. allow

_____ **7.** hostile
    a. friendly   c. eager
    b. argumentative   d. alone

_____ **8.** belligerent
    a. serious   c. noisy
    b. peaceful   d. combative

_____ **9.** sarcastic
    a. nasty   c. flattering
    b. cutting   d. silent

_____ **10.** ponderous
    a. heavy   c. fancy
    b. light   d. obvious

EXERCISE **3** Fill in the Blank

Use context clues to determine the word that best completes each sentence.

1. When Billy Collins was named the U.S. Poet Laureate in 2001, some people complained because they thought poetry should be _____ and difficult to understand, and they argued that Collins's poems were too light and simple.

2. A _____ remark to persons of authority would be viewed as disrespectful, so we should reflect on our word choices and avoid speaking hastily.

3. A technical foul was called on the home team during a basketball game because many of the fans were _____ the visiting team with unkind remarks.

4. The defense acknowledged the _____ witness, one who was called because of her expert opinion, but who could also endanger the case because she knew too much through doctor/patient privilege.

5. The _____ customer annoyed the salesman, who still managed to remain calm and polite.

6. We listened as the motivational speaker _____ inspiration and wisdom, communicating ideas that generated confidence in the audience.

7. Because we live in a visual society, presidential candidates must create an image that causes voters to _____ them as strong, attractive, charming, confident leaders.

8. Under the full moon, _____ of the pumpkin vine cast corkscrew shadows against the picket fence.

9. Kyle was worried by the _____ of his girlfriend's voice when she said, "We need to talk."

10. Cyril Connolly used a poor filing system as a _____ for our imperfect memory when he said, "Our memories are card indexes consulted and then returned in disorder by authorities whom we do not control."

EXERCISE 4 Application

Using context clues, insert the vocabulary word in the appropriate blank. A part-of-speech clue is given for each vocabulary word.

Why is it that just when I try to change, new challenges present themselves and make life more difficult? William thought about this question as he considered the recent events with his friends. As long as he was willing to hang with the crowd, **(1)** (v.) _____ and bully people who were different from themselves, and choose to adopt a **(2)** (adj.) _____, mean-spirited attitude, his friends were happy. However, when he tried to do the right thing, they became **(3)** (adj.) _____, criticizing his actions as weak. They **(4)** (v.) _____ William as a coward if he used a respectful **(5)** (n.) _____ with an authority figure rather than a **(6)** (adj.) _____ one. If he tried to **(7)** (v.) _____ wisdom, they viewed him as **(8)** (adj.) _____ and dreary—no longer fun-loving and light-hearted. William knew that for a long time his group was, for him, a **(9)** (n.) _____ for a family—a community to which he felt he belonged. Now, however, after watching the destruction and pain they were causing in the neighborhood, he realized they were the ones who were weak and afraid—fearful of acting on their own. With his new choice to act independently of his crowd, William at first felt like a slender

(10) (n.) _____, struggling to cling to a different branch. In his

heart, however, he felt his choice was a good one, albeit lonely, and eventually

he would grow stronger and more autonomous.

Stop and Think

Go to **http://www.loc.gov/poetry/180/** and select a poem. In the space below, write a 30-word summary that includes your interpretation of the tone of the poem.

_____

_____

_____

Try some imitative poetry. Fill in the blanks with your own choices, so that the reader can discover something about yourself through your tone.

I'm a _____ in _____ syllables.

An _____, a _____ _____.

A _____ _____ing on _____ _____.

0 _____ _____, _____, fine _____!

This _____'s big with its _____ _____.

_____'s new-_____ in this _____ _____.

I'm a _____s, a _____, a _____ in _____.

I've _____ a _____ of _____ _____s,

_____. There's no getting off.

—Farina, Deborah. Scaffolding Writing Lecture at The College of William and Mary, April 2006. Reprinted by permission of Deborah Farina.

22 Vocabulary and Nonfiction Literature

Get Ready to Read About Nonfiction Literature

Nonfiction literature includes pieces such as essays, biographies, autobiographies, and memoirs—works that are true. Unlike fiction, in which the content is created in the author's imagination, nonfiction chronicles factual events, although the details may be filtered through the author's memory, which may sometimes be flawed. Below is the introduction to *A Night to Remember*, a book that details the events of the night the *Titanic* sank. Sometimes, to appreciate nonfiction, an effective reader needs to recognize ironic events such as the ones presented here. Before you read this selection, recall what you already know about the following word parts.

1. The prefix *con-* means *with, together.*

2. The prefix *dis-* means _____.

3. The prefix *re-* means _____.

4. The root *plac* means *peace.*

collectively	concoct	fictional	irony	titan
complacent	displacement	futility	maiden	vessel

IRONY AND REAL LIFE

When readers first encounter the introduction to William Lord's *A Night to Remember*, they scratch their heads and wonder at the **irony** of the descriptions of the two ships, one fictional, one real. In fact, one reader recently asked, "How do you account for this? Parallel universes, maybe?" Read the author's comparison to draw your own conclusion.

FOREWORD

In 1898 a struggling author named Morgan Robertson **concocted** a novel about a fabulous Atlantic liner, far larger than any that had ever been built. Robertson loaded his ship with rich and **complacent** people and then wrecked it one cold April night on an iceberg. This somehow showed the **futility** of everything, and in fact, the book was called *Futility* when it appeared that year, published by the firm of M.F. Mansfield.

Fourteen years later a British shipping company named the White Star Line built a steamer remarkably like the one in Robertson's novel. The new liner was 66,000 tons **displacement;** Robertson's was 70,000. The real ship was 882.5 feet long; the **fictional** one was 800 feet. Both **vessels** were triple screw and could make 24–25 knots. Both could carry about 3,000 people, and both had enough lifeboats for only a fraction of this number. But, then, this didn't seem to matter because both were labeled "unsinkable."

On April 10, 1912, the real ship left Southampton on her **maiden** voyage to New York. Her cargo included a priceless copy of the *Rubáiyát of Omar Khayyám* and a list of passengers **collectively** worth two hundred fifty million dollars. On her way over she too struck an iceberg and went down on a cold April night.

Robertson called his ship the *Titan*; the White Star Line called its ship the *Titanic.*

—Excerpt from Foreword from *A Night to Remember* by Walter Lord, © 1955, 1983 by Walter Lord. Reprinted by permission of Henry Holt and Company, LLC.

VISUAL VOCABULARY

Sister ship to the *Titanic*, the

Olympic sailed on her _____ voyage on December 11, 1915.

a. maiden
b. complacent

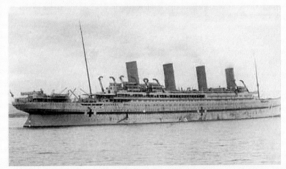

Source: http://www.starway.org/Titanic/Sister_Ships.html
retrieved 01/13/06

EXERCISE 1 Context Clues

Refer to the previous passage and use context clues from the sentences below to determine the definition of each of the following words in **bold** print. Do not consult a dictionary.

1. collectively (kə-lĕk′tĭv-lē′) adv.
   After much discussion, the student body **collectively** agreed to have a fundraiser and invite the former president to be a guest lecturer.

   _____ **Collectively** means
       a. partly.   c. totally.
       b. selectively.   d. uniformly.

2. complacent (kəm-plā′sənt) adj.
   Students were recently cautioned about becoming **complacent** and too comfortable while walking across campus alone at night; instead, they should be careful and make plans to travel in pairs.

   _____ **Complacent** means
       a. in trouble.   c. confused.
       b. insecure.   d. too confident.

3. concoct (kən-kŏkt′) v.
   Amy **concocted** a meal based on a recipe of Puerco Pibil that she saw demonstrated at the end of the Johnny Depp DVD, _Once Upon a Time in Mexico_.

   _____ **Concoct** means
       a. think up; prepare.   c. divide.
       b. unmix.   d. ruin.

4. displacement (dĭs-plās′mənt) n.
   A modern-day aircraft carrier has a **displacement** of 91,209 tons versus a World War II carrier, which was 23,927 tons.

   _____ **Displacement** means
       a. admission.   c. length.
       b. employment.   d. weight or volume of a fluid shifted by a solid.

5. fictional (fĭk′shən əl) adj.
   Tim Burton's _Big Fish_ is about a man who is suspected of telling his son **fictional** stories about his life.

   _____ **Fictional** means
       a. authentic.   c. imaginary.
       b. passionate.   d. unknown.

6. futility (fyoō-tǐl′ǐ-tē) n.
David complained about the **futility** of trying to rake leaves during a 50 mph windstorm.

_____ **Futility** means
   a. uselessness.
   b. organization.
   c. imagination.
   d. importance.

7. irony (ī′rə-nē) n.
The master of **irony,** O. Henry was known for short stories with surprise endings such as "The Last Leaf," which is about an artist who dies after painting a leaf on a window pane for a young woman in his apartment building, after she announces that she will die when the last leaf falls from the tree outside.

_____ **Irony** means
   a. literary style with an unexpected twist.
   b. horror.
   c. literary style with an expected ending.
   d. prediction.

8. maiden (mād′n) adj.
After a ship is built, it will go through "shakedown," which consists of builders' trials; then after the owner's acceptance, it will go on its **maiden** voyage.

_____ **Maiden** means
   a. recent.
   b. first.
   c. last.
   d. tragic.

9. titan (tīt′n) n.
Bill Gates is known as a **titan** in the field of computer technology.

_____ **Titan** means
   a. giant.
   b. miniature.
   c. failure.
   d. monster.

10. vessel (vĕs′əl) n.
Cities are often built near rivers that are waterways for the **vessels** that provide transportation for people and products as well as furnish a form of self-defense.

_____ **Vessel** means
   a. bridge.
   b. water vehicle.
   c. road vehicle.
   d. aircraft.

EXERCISE 2 Word Sorts

Synonyms

Match the word to the synonyms or definitions that follow each blank.

1. _____ boat; barge; craft; bark

2. _____ brew; cook up; create; conjure

3. _____ beginning; first; original; initial

4. _____ paradox; incongruity; twist; contradiction

5. _____ weight shifted by fluid of a floating body

Antonyms

Select the letter of the word(s) with the opposite meaning.

_____ **6.** titan
   a. star
   b. dwarf
   c. rumor
   d. triumph

_____ **7.** futility
   a. usefulness
   b. uselessness
   c. seriousness
   d. imagination

_____ **8.** fictional
   a. imagined
   b. fabled
   c. authentic
   d. inspirational

_____ **9.** collectively
   a. altogether
   b. all told
   c. bodily
   d. individually

_____ **10.** complacent
   a. dissatisfied
   b. contented
   c. easy-going
   d. calm

EXERCISE 3 Fill in the Blank

Use context clues to determine the word that best completes each sentence.

1. After the _____ flight of *Space Ship One*, the team won the $10 million Ansari X Prize that promotes the development of commercial flight into space because it successfully launched a vehicle at an altitude of 62.14 miles with three people on board.

2. Heidi worried about her sons' safety when she learned they had

   _____ a scheme to sail a homemade raft in the unpredictable waters known as the "Graveyard of the Atlantic."

3. Imagine the _____ Susan and George experienced when they gave each other the same Christmas present after dating only two weeks.

4. At six foot ten inches, the basketball center was a _____, even in the midst of most of the other very tall players.

5. Growth is impossible when a person becomes _____ and too comfortable, choosing to sit back calmly rather than aiming for new goals.

6. In order to allow _____ to travel in deep water, bridges must be built high enough or constructed with the feature that allows a span to lift or rotate.

7. Until she received some career counseling, Sula had felt only

   _____ when she realized her major was no longer in a field in which she was interested.

8. The NCAA coach accepted the honor of coach of the year; however, he

   said it really _____ belonged to the players and his staff, who made him look so good.

9. Many films that claim to be based on a true story are actually

   _____ if little of the final movie resembles the actual events.

10. When filling a beverage in a glass, be sure to leave room for the

    _____ of the ice cubes.

EXERCISE 4 Application

Using context clues, insert the vocabulary word in the appropriate blank. A part-of-speech clue is given for each vocabulary word.

Sam and Natasha shivered by the fire, sipping from mugs of steaming coffee, feeling relieved and calm after the recent unsettling events. The

(1) (n.) _____ of the outcome with its unexpected ending actually brought smiles to the young couple's faces.

Sam had sold his motorcycle because Natasha had decided it was no longer safe following a close call Sam had experienced one sunny afternoon. He had been too **(2)** (adj.) _____ about the traffic and failed to be alert to potential dangers. He had almost been killed by a driver running a red light.

After that day, Sam talked about his dream of buying a sailboat big enough to live on and travel the seas. Natasha immediately realized the **(3)** (n.) _____ of trying to dissuade a determined man, so she allowed him to pursue his interest.

With the profit from the sale of the motorcycle and their savings, they had purchased a sailboat and spent the next few months refurbishing it. Considering the time, materials, and furnishings, their investment was now **(4)** (adv.) _____ worth nearly $50,000. And it was a beauty with the scarlet Genoa sail, teak deck, and plush interior. Also, with a **(5)** (n.) _____ of three tons, it was very seaworthy.

Sam and Natasha **(6)** (v.) _____ the idea of living on the boat after seeing a movie, which was a **(7)** (adj.) _____ story about two people who sailed the world alone in a similar **(8)** (n.) _____. It seemed romantic at the time.

Now, here they were huddled by the fire, soaked, after only a few hours in the water on their **(9)** (adj.) _____ voyage on the boat. It seems they misjudged the weather, which can change drastically in the area. What promised to be a good day rapidly changed to gale-force winds. Fortunately, excellent sailing lessons and quick thinking had saved them both as well as their sailboat. In Natasha's eyes, Sam was a **(10)** (n.) _____ in the world of husbands, standing well above the others in comparison. It was his quick thinking that had saved them.

Safer, indeed, thought Natasha.

Their plan now is to sail only with, as the expert sailors say, "Fair winds and following seas."

Stop and Think

 Pyramid Summary: Choose one word from this chapter and complete the pyramid summary below. You may consult your dictionary for additional help.

1. Word
2. Synonym
3. Antonym
4. Etymology
5. Sentence

1. _____

    2. _____

  3. _____

4. _____

5. _____

 Go to **www.wikipedia.com** and search titan mythology. Read about the gods of Greek mythology who were titans. Then study the drawing below and write a caption.

Molly Gamble-Walker

_____
_____
_____
_____
_____
_____
_____
_____
_____

Review Test
Chapters 18–22

1 Word Parts

Match the definitions in Column 2 to the word parts in Column 1.

Column 1

_____ **1.** ambi-

_____ **2.** path

_____ **3.** arch

_____ **4.** phob

_____ **5.** epi-

_____ **6.** –ize

_____ **7.** mur

_____ **8.** nasci

_____ **9.** belli

_____ **10.** xeno

Column 2

a. war

b. both

c. wall

d. feeling

e. cause to become

f. first; leader

g. fear

h. strange; foreign

i. around

j. to be born

2 Fill in the Blank

Use context clues to determine the best word from the box to complete each sentence.

ambiguity	concoct	intercultural	metaphor	sarcastic
belligerent	ethnocentrism	irony	ponderous	tendril

1. "There was so much _____ in the film that I just didn't understand whether it was supposed to be a drama, a mystery, or a comedy," remarked Jesse as he left the theater with a confused look.

2. Because of _____, people in some cultures view Americans as cold and uncaring if they put their elderly in nursing homes, while Latinos, who care for extended family members into old age, are viewed as warm and compassionate.

3. Today there are more _____ exchange programs available to college students who want to study abroad or participate in a community outreach program in another country.

4. Until he discovered his talent in cycling, Lance Armstrong had a reputation as a young man of being _____, argumentative, and difficult with some people.

5. In addition to being a good story, *Where the Heart Is* by Billie Letts also uses the journey theme as a _____ that compares life to a trip along which her main character Novalee Nation meets people who provide her with opportunities, shelter, wisdom, and advice that she needs.

6. One of the most _____ and hurtful comments a friend can make to someone who is facing difficulty is, "That sounds like a personal problem to me."

7. Despite the imaginative excuse Brett _____ for the security officer who caught him jumping the wall of the Governor's Palace, he was banned from the restored area and never allowed to visit any of the other museums or restaurants in the area.

8. There are several types of _____ that originate on different parts of plants.

9. The mood was _____ and heavy when the football quarterback discovered no one had drafted him to play for the NFL.

5

10. A favorite classic film that has a twist of _____ is *The Sting*, in which the ruthless gangster is outwitted several times by the main characters, and their revenge begins to look like justice.

3 Book Connection

Use context clues to determine the best word from the box to complete each sentence. A part-of-speech clue is provided for each vocabulary word.

augment	hamper	pioneering	stereotype	tolerate
epitomize	incremental	precipitate	taunt	tone

COPY THIS!

Paul Orfalea (pronounced or-fa-la) begins his autobiographical book by explaining how he became a multimillionaire without really reading. Yes, you read that correctly. Although he was diagnosed as a hyperactive dyslexic, Orfalea has an amazing success story. He **(1)** (v.) _____ the person who overcomes great odds and eventually triumphs.

The story is told with wit and a self-deprecating humorous **(2)** (n.) _____. As a child, Orfalea quickly discovered that his inability to learn in conventional ways **(3)** (v.) _____ him academically. What amazed him, though, was that he was not at the bottom of his class when he graduated from high school. His grades were poor, and he often exhibited behavior that would not be **(4)** (v.) _____ in public schools. Private schools, however, could not help him either.

Although observers often **(5)** (v.) _____ students with learning disabilities as lazy troublemakers, Orfalea's story dispels that myth. In fact, even though some people report that their learning disabilities crushed them, especially if they were **(6)** (v.) _____ by classmates, others learned to compensate and overcome the obstacle. For Orfalea, the latter was his experience, especially because he had a mother who said she believed in his genius and his ability to succeed.

Do you know yet what his successful business venture was? Think Kinko's. In fact, the name of his business was the nickname Orfalea developed as a result of his curly red hair. A **(7)** (adj.) _____ businessman, he started one small copy center and then expanded to several. Although it was not an overnight success, Kinko's grew in **(8)** (adj.) _____ steps until it eventually became a multimillion dollar business. One secret of his success, Orfalea explains in his book, is that he supported the tenet that you value your co-workers and reward them. Along with that principle, he also believes in studying what works and modeling other centers after those good practices. He also avoided holding business meetings. Finally, he hired good people who could fill in where he has learning gaps.

Copy This! is a book that inspires and reminds readers that a disability can **(9)** (v.) _____ an opportunity. Although Orfalea has sold his business to FEDEX and **(10)** (v.) _____ his savings with a huge profit, he continues to motivate others through lectures and teaching opportunities. It is another irony of life that he became a college lecturer who teaches good business practices to future business leaders.

4 Visual Connection

Write a caption for this picture using two words from the box.

Elizabeth Pongratz

_____
_____
_____
_____
_____
_____

5 Analogies

Choose the word that best completes the analogy.

accord	complacent	displacement	infringement	perceive
assumption	deterioration	impart	maiden	tenuous

1. sow : harvest :: get rid of : _____
   a. perceive   b. accumulate   c. tolerate

2. telephone: conference call :: classroom : _____
   a. interaction   b. accumulate   c. tolerate

3. anger : disagreement :: despair: _____
   a. futility   b. irony   c. groundwork

4. friend : dishonest :: witness : _____
   a. fictional   b. maiden   c. hostile

5. canvas : painting :: wall : _____
   a. mural   b. sculpture   c. deterioration

6. roof : summit :: foundation : _____
   a. tenet   b. tendril   c. groundwork

7. criminal : condemn :: hero : _____
   a. tolerate   b. celebrate   c. perceive

8. dancer : graceful :: robot : _____
   a. complacent   b. intolerable   c. mechanized

9. person : individually :: group : _____
   a. tenuously   b. ponderously   c. collectively

10. teach : instruct:: divulge : _____
   a. disclose   b. stereotype   c. taunt

APPENDIX

A

Word Parts

Roots

Root	Meaning	Example
alter	change	altercation
ama	love	amorous
anima	breath, spirit	animated
anno	year	annual
aqua	water	aquifer
aster, astro	star	asteroid
aud	hear	auditory
bene	good	beneficial
bio	life	biology
cap	head	decapitate
cap, capt	take	captivate
card, cor, cord	heart	cardiologist, core
ced, ceed, cess	go	proceed
cosmo	order, universe	cosmos
cresc	grow, increase	crescendo
cryp	secret, hidden	crypt
dent	tooth	dentist
derm	skin	epidermis
dict	say	predict
duc, duct	lead, guide	conductor
dynam	power	dynamic
ego	self	egotistical
equ, equal	equal	equilibrium
err, errat	wander	erratic
ethno	race, tribe	ethnic
fac, fact	do, make	factory
fer	carry	transfer
flu, fluct, flux	flow	influx
fract	break	fracture

235

Root	Meaning	Example
frater	brother	fraternal
gene	race, kind, sex	genetics
grad, gres	go, take, steps	graduate
graph	write, draw	autograph
gyn	woman	gynecologist
hab, habi	have, hold	habitat
hap	change	happenstance
helio	sun, light	heliograph
ject	throw	eject
lat	carry	translate
lic, liqu, list	leave behind	liquidate
lith	stone	monolith
loc	place	relocate
log	speech, science, reason	logic
loquor	speak	colloquial
lumen, lumin	light	luminary
macro	large	macroeconomics
manu	hand	manual
mater	mother	maternal
med	middle	mediator
meter	measure	thermometer
micro	small	microorganism
miss, mit	send, let go	transmit
morph	form	morpheme
mort	die	mortal
mot, mov	movement	demote
mul, muta	change	mutation
nat	be born	natural, native
neg, negat	say no, deny	negate, negative
nomen, nym	name	antonym, synonym
pel, puls	push, drive	propel
philo	love	philanthropy
ocul	eye	monocle
ortho	right, straight	orthodontist
osteo	bone	osteoporosis
pater	father	paternal
path	suffering, feeling	pathology

Root	Meaning	Example
ped	child	pediatrician
ped, pod	foot	podiatrist
phobia	fear	claustrophobia
phon	sound	telephone
photo	light	photograph
plic	fold	implicate
pneuma	wind, air	pneumonia
pon, pos, posit	put, place	dispose
port	carry	import
pseudo	false	pseudonym
psych	mind	psychology
press	press	compress
pyr	fire	pyromaniac
quir, quis	ask	inquire
rog	question	interrogate
scope	see	microscope
scrib, script	write	inscription
sect	cut	dissect
sequi	follow	sequence
sol	alone	solitude
soma	body	somatotype
somnia	sleep	insomnia
soph	wise	sophisticated
soror	sister	sorority
spect	look	inspect
spers	scatter	disperse
spir	breathe	inspire
struct	build	construction
tact	touch	tactile
tain, tent	hold	contain
tempo	time	temporary
the, theo	God	theology
therm	heat	thermometer
tort	twist	contort
tract	drag, pull	extract
verbum	word	verbatim
vis	see	revise

Prefixes

Prefix	Meaning	Example
a-, ab-	away, from	abduct
a-, an-	not, without	asexual
ac-, ad-	to, toward	accept, admit
ambi-, amphi-	both, around	ambivalent, amphitheater
ante-	in front of, before	antecedent
anti-	against, oppose	antisocial
auto-	self	automatic
bi-	two, twice	bifocal
cata-, cath-	down, downward	catacombs
cent-	hundred	centennial
chrono-	time	chronological
circum-	around	circumspect
col-, com-, con-	with, together	collate, combine, connection
contra-	against	contradict
de-	down away, reversal	destruction
deca-	ten	decade
demi-	half	demigod
di-, duo-	two	dioxide
dia-	between, through	diagonal, dialogue
dis-	apart, away, in different directions	dismiss
dys-	ill, hard	dysfunctional
e-, ex-	out, from	emerge, expel
epi-	on, near, among	epidemic
eu-	good	euphoric
extra-	beyond, outside	extramarital
hecto-	hundred	hectogram
hemi-	half	hemisphere
hetero-	other, different	heterosexual
homo-	same	homonym
hyper-	above, excessive	hyperactive
hypo-	under	hypodermic
il-, im-, in-	not	illogical, impossible

Prefix	Meaning	Example
im-, in-	in, into, on	implant, inject
infra-	lower	infrastructure
inter-	between, among	intercede
intra-	within	intranet
iso-	equal	isometric
juxta-	next to	juxtapose
mal-	wrong, ill	malpractice
meta-	about	metaphysical
micro-	small	microscope
mil-	thousand	millennium
mis-	wrong	mistake
mono-	one	monotone
multi-	many	multimedia
non-	not	nonactive
nona-	nine	nonagon
octo-	eight	octopus
omni-	all	omniscient
pan-	all	panorama
penta-	five	pentagram
per-	through	pervade
peri-	around	periscope
poly-	many	polygon
post-	after, behind	postscript
pre-	before	precede
pro-	forward, on behalf of	promote
proto-	first	prototype
quadri-	four	quadrant
quint-	five	quintuplets
re-	back, again	retract
retro-	backward	retrospect
semi-	half	semicircle
sesqui-	one and a half	sesquicentennial
sex-	six	sextet
sub-, sup-	under, from below	subgroup, support
super-	above, over, beyond	supervise

Prefix	Meaning	Example
sym-, syn-	together, with	symmetry, synonym
tele-	far, from a distance	telegraph
tetra-	four	tetrahedron
trans-	across	transport
tri-	three	triangle, triplet
ultra-	excessive, beyond	ultrasonic
un-	not	unnecessary
uni-	one	uniform
vice-	in place of	viceroy

Suffixes

Suffix	Meaning	Example
Noun suffixes	*People, places, thing*	
-acle, -acy, -ance	quality, state	privacy
-an	of, related to	American
-ant, -ary	one who, one that	servant
-arium, -ary	place or container	auditorium
-ation	action, process	education
-ator	one who	spectator
-cide	kill	homicide
-eer, -er, -ess	person, doer	collector
-ence, -ency	quality, state	residence, residency
-ent	one who, one that	president
-hood	quality, condition, state	brotherhood
-ician	specialist	statistician
-ism	belief	modernism
-ist	person	extremist
-ity	quality, trait	sincerity
-logy	study of	biology
-ment	act, state	statement
-ness	quality, condition, state	illness
-or	person, doer	juror
-path	practitioner; sufferer of a disorder	osteopath; psychopath

Suffix	Meaning	Example
-ship	quality, condition, state	relationship
-tion	action, state	fraction
-tude	quality, degree	multitude
-y	quality, trait	apathy

Adjective suffixes	*Descriptions of nouns*	
-able	capable of	reusable
-ac, -al, -an, -ar, -ative	of, like, related to, being	logical
-ent	of, like, related to, being	persistent
-ful	full of	fearful
-ible	capable of	defensible
-ic, -ical, -ile, -ious, -ish, -ive	of, like, related to, being	feverish
-less	without	luckless

APPENDIX

B

Foreign Words and Phrases

While many words in your dictionary evolved from Greek and Latin word parts, some words have remained intact from their original form. These foreign words and phrases will appear in your everyday use as well as in some academic settings.

French

1. coup d'etat (ko͞o′ dā-tä′) n. [blow, stroke of state] violent or illegal overthrow of those authority in the government

2. faux pas (fō pä′) n. [false step] a social mistake

3. nom de plume (nŏm′ də plo͞om′) n. [pen name] a pseudonym or pen name a writer uses

Latin

4. ad infinitum (ăd ĭn′fə-nī′təm) adv. & adj. [to infinity] having no end

5. bona fide (bō′nə fīd′) adj. [good faith] genuine; sincere

6. esprit de corps (ĕ-sprē-də kôr′) n. [spirit of the body] cooperative spirit; morale

Italian

7. vendetta (vĕn-dĕt′ə) n. [revenge] a blood feud

Spanish

8. aficionado (a-fĭsh′-ē-ə-nä′-dō) an admirer or follower; a fan

9. conquistador (kŏn-kwĭs′tə-dôr′, kŏng-kē′stə-) n. [to conquer] a conqueror, especially a 16th century Spanish soldier

10. flotilla (flō-tĭl′ə) n. [fleet] a small fleet of small vessels

Partial Answer Key

Chapter 1

Exercise 1A

1. _b_
2. _c_
3. _d_
4. _a_
5. _a_

Exercise 2A

1. _c_
2. _b_
3. _a_
4. _d_
5. _a_

Exercise 3A

1. _c_
2. _a_
3. _b_
4. _a_
5. _c_

Exercise 4A

1. _d_
2. _c_
3. _a_
4. _b_
5. _c_

Exercise 5A

1. _b_
2. _c_
3. _a_
4. _c_
5. _d_

Chapter 3

1. _d_
2. _b_
3. _b_
4. _a_
5. _b_
6. _b_

7. _c_
8. _a_
9. _d_
10. _b_

Chapter 4

1. _a_
2. _b_
3. _a_
4. _c_
5. _b_
6. _a_
7. _c_
8. _d_
9. _c_
10. _c_

Chapter 5

1. _b_
2. _d_
3. _a_

4. _c_
5. _a_
6. _d_
7. _c_
8. _a_
9. _d_
10. _b_

Chapter 6

1. _c_
2. _b_
3. _a_
4. _c_
5. _a_
6. _d_
7. _b_
8. _b_
9. _b_
10. _d_

Chapter 7

1. b
2. d
3. a
4. c
5. a
6. a
7. b
8. b
9. a
10. c

Chapter 8

1. c
2. d
3. a
4. a
5. d
6. a
7. b
8. a
9. d
10. b

Chapter 9

1. b
2. a
3. b
4. b
5. d

6. c
7. b
8. a
9. c
10. b

Chapter 10

1. d
2. a
3. b
4. c
5. a
6. b
7. a
8. b
9. b
10. c

Chapter 11

1. a
2. c
3. b
4. b
5. a
6. d
7. b
8. a
9. c
10. b

Chapter 12

1. a
2. c
3. d
4. b
5. c
6. a
7. d
8. a
9. a
10. d

Chapter 13

1. c
2. c
3. d
4. a
5. a
6. c
7. d
8. b
9. c
10. d

Chapter 14

1. c
2. d
3. a
4. d

Chapter 15

1. d
2. c
3. b
4. c
5. a
6. a
7. d
8. a
9. b
10. b

Chapter 16

1. a
2. c
3. a
4. b
5. b
6. d
7. c
8. c
9. a
10. b

Chapter 17
1. c
2. b
3. d
4. a
5. a
6. b
7. c
8. b
9. c
10. d

Chapter 18
1. a
2. b
3. d
4. b
5. c
6. d
7. a
8. b
9. a
10. c

Chapter 19
1. a
2. b
3. a
4. c
5. a
6. a
7. c
8. d
9. a
10. d

Chapter 20
1. b
2. b
3. c
4. d
5. a
6. b
7. c
8. d
9. a
10. a

Chapter 21
1. b
2. c
3. b
4. a
5. d
6. c
7. d
8. a
9. d
10. d

Chapter 22
1. c
2. d
3. a
4. d
5. c
6. a
7. a
8. b
9. a
10. b